Assessing Students' Digital Writing

Assessing Students' Digital Writing

Protocols for Looking Closely

Edited by **Troy Hicks**

Foreword by Richard Beach
Prologue by Christina Cantrill, National Writing Project

TEACHERS COLLEGE PRESS
TEACHERS COLLEGE | COLUMBIA UNIVERSITY
NEW YORK AND LONDON

National Writing Project
Berkeley, CA

Published simultaneously by Teachers College Press, 1234 Amsterdam Avenue, New York, NY 10027 and the National Writing Project, 2105 Bancroft Way, Berkeley, CA 94720-1042.

The National Writing Project (NWP) is a nationwide network of educators working together to improve the teaching of writing in the nation's schools and in other settings. NWP provides high-quality professional development programs to teachers in a variety of disciplines and at all levels, from early childhood through university. Through its network of nearly 200 university-based sites, NWP develops the leadership, programs, and research needed for teachers to help students become successful writers and learners.

Library of Congress Cataloging-in-Publication Data

Assessing students' digital writing : protocols for looking closely / edited by Troy
   Hicks ; foreword by Christina Cantril.
       pages cm
   Includes bibliographical references and index.
   ISBN 978-0-8077-5669-0 (pbk. : alk. paper)
   ISBN 978-0-8077-7387-1 (e-book)
       1. English language—Composition and exercises—Computer-assisted
   instruction. 2. English language—Composition and exercises—Study and
   teaching—Evaluation. I. Hicks, Troy, editor of compilation.
   LB1576.7.A77 2015
   372.60785—dc23   2015005714

ISBN 978-0-8077-5669-0 (paper)
ISBN 978-0-8077-7387-1 (ebook)

Printed on acid-free paper
Manufactured in the United States of America

22   21   20   19   18   17   16   15   8   7   6   5   4   3   2   1

To the teacher leaders of the National Writing Project:

Hey, we make 40 look great!
Here is to our next four decades together.

—TH

Contents

Foreword

This timely book addresses a major challenge for teachers needing to know how to give feedback on digital writing that is multimodal, interactive, intertextual, employs combined/remixed images/video, is geared for public audiences, and is collaboratively constructed. Providing useful feedback on these features of digital writing entails focusing not only on the digital products, but also on the processes involved in creating these productions.

Through six engaging case studies, we experience teachers' innovative uses of a range of tools to foster digital writing. Each of the teachers documents how they created audience, purpose, and situation-constituting contexts mediated by uses of digital tools to motivate their students writing. Given these contexts, the teachers then describe how they assessed their students' processes for engaging their audiences; for example, how Kaplan and Zangerle's students created PSA videos to achieve positive uptake from their audiences.

In doing so, the teachers were assessing students' ability to contextualize how their digital texts resonated with their peer-group, school, or larger community audiences. For example, Puntel's students created a video game involving a "teach-in" as a part of her social justice and multicultural ethics course, which required students to consider how to engage audiences in critical inquiry about issues of justice and ethics. Given that context, her feedback focused on students' ability to empathize with their own and others' roles.

The case studies illustrate the need to integrate the understanding of effective use of features of digital texts with employing those features in creating digital texts. To create their book review trailers, Hyler's students studied examples of trailers. To create informational text on a website, Johnson's students studied the Wonderopolis website. In doing so, students gained an understanding of the effective use of the following features of digital writing:

- *Multimodality.* Students perceived how digital writing meshes images, videos, audio, and language; for example, how West-Puckett's student Zeke created his stop-motion animation by combining images with sound and music. Students' multimodal productions also employed what Hicks described as the "both-and" use of both print and digital writing; for example, Kaplan and Zangerle's students writing a script for their PSA videos leading to assessing how print texts support digital production.
- *Intertextuality.* In contrast to autonomous print-based texts, the students' digital writing included links to other texts, entailing assessment of how use of these links effectively builds on and leads to other texts to enhance understanding of a topic or theme.
- *Interactivity.* Students' digital texts served to foster interactivity between students and texts. When Klein's 2nd-grade students used the Aurasma app to create videos linked to images of their reports, other students could then hold their devices up to those words in order to view these videos, suggesting assessment of how this interaction with texts enhances engagement.
- *Combining/remixing images/video.* Klein's students also used digital tools such as Glogster to combine and remix images, leading to assessing how these combinations or remixes of images/videos recontextualize the meaning of these images or videos to create new meanings.
- *Geared for public audiences.* Students were creating texts for public audiences beyond the classroom, leading teachers to consider students' awareness of their audiences' knowledge and needs.
- *Collaboration.* Students employed digital tools such as VoiceThread to share their collaborative responses to texts, involving assessment of students' ability to work collaboratively with one another.

The book therefore demonstrates the need for a major shift in how teachers assess students' digital writing based on features that can differ from those of print texts, particularly in terms of providing descriptive feedback regarding students' processes involved in creating digital texts.

These case studies also aptly illustrate how contextualizing uses of digital texts involves more than simply adhering to criteria associated with an assigned, predetermined context. Through uses of digital tools, students were engaged in what Chris Gallagher (2014) describes as performing contexts through creating interfaces or relationships between themselves and their audiences in often unpredictable, evolving ways. The teachers then recognized the limitation of using predetermined, fixed assessment criteria versus criteria consistent with how students' use of these tools evolved over time, as evident in how Hyler altered his criteria for the book review trailer productions based on what his students actually created.

This book also documents the value of teachers' collaborative online sharing of perceptions about their students' digital writing practices, which led them to engage in thoughtful self-reflection about their teaching and their students' digital writing, serving as a model for groups of teachers interested in improving their teaching through online interaction.

—Richard Beach, Professor Emeritus, University of Minnesota

Prologue

An Introduction to the National Writing Project's "Digital Is" Website

> The teacher in revolutionary mode . . . sees and responds to each child
> as a work of art.
>
> —Pat Carini (Sarah Lawrence College, 2011)

Many years ago I was introduced to the idea of looking closely, and describing carefully, the work that youth were creating by Judy Buchanan, then one of the directors of the Philadelphia Writing Project (PhilWP). I remember a day when Judy was getting ready to share student work and a related process of oral inquiry, or "descriptive review," at the PhilWP Summer Institute. She had been actively collecting—and learning in-depth from—the work of one of her students named Anwar (Buchanan, 1994). She also had a collection of another student's work from the Prospect School in Vermont; this collection spanned the course of one student's entire school career. These and other collections were made available for loan to other educators.

It was astounding to see all of a student's work pulled together in this way. "Wow, look at all there is to see," I remember thinking. However, it wasn't until the next day at the Institute, when I actually saw Judy and the other teachers engage with the work in a descriptive way—talking about what they saw while withholding judgment, critique, analysis, and evaluation—that the educator/organizer part of my brain was triggered. It was clear to me then, as it is clear to me now, that learning from student work in this way is where teaching should be centered and informed.

Fast-forward many years, and educators across the National Writing Project (NWP) network continue to do active inquiry alongside their students, and with one another, too. Increasingly, they do this with new tools and technologies and via expanded online networks and communities. Whether youth are blogging and connecting across the country at Youth Voices (youthvoices.net) or creating multimedia/transmedia work and sharing it via social media, the process of looking at what youth are producing—and actively engaging in inquiry around those productions—is a key way that writing project teachers continue to learn together.

Inspired by what educators were noticing when students were engaging with new networked tools and technologies, the NWP, through support from the MacArthur Foundation's Digital Media and Learning Initiative, organized the Digital Is... conference in 2009. This conference brought together a group of educators who spanned grades and disciplines, as well as those who worked outside of schools. We asked ourselves the question: If *digital is* the way that we write, communicate, share, and engage today, what does that mean for learning and for teaching?

And we set about answering this by looking closely at student work again, much as many of us had studied the work of children previously. However, this time, we were looking at digital artifacts, at work that was often created collaboratively by multiple students, with tools we weren't necessarily familiar with ourselves, published in a range of media intended for audiences that we didn't even know, and inspired and supported in spaces and places that weren't necessarily school. But in taking the time to look closely, we started to understand what was really happening in and across classrooms, maker spaces, youth development programs, after-school clubs, and virtual online spaces, and when youth connect on their own time. From there, we began to imagine how we might build better and more connected learning ecosystems to support the growth and development of these kinds of work for all young learners.

The NWP's Digital Is website (digitalis.nwp.org), then, is one of the ecosystems we began to build out of these conversations. It is a place where we publish and learn as professionals, and it features work shared by educators across disciplines, grades, and contexts. It was established as an open website where work is added in an ongoing way with the explicit intention of focusing on how connected learning and literacy are changing in our increasingly digital world. We continue to build and imagine this work today (with, for instance, initiatives like Educator Innovator [educatorinnovator. org]), and this ethos is also what the teacher writers in this collection demonstrate.

NWP therefore is privileged and honored to collaborate with Troy, Erin, Julie, Jeremy, Bonnie, Jack, Christina, Stephanie, and Teachers College Press to host the student work and related artifacts that have emerged out of this group's thoughtful, groundbreaking, and yes, revolutionary, work. Readers can follow the links and QR codes to see the students' work in its original, digital format, leave comments for its authors, share it with others, and even publish new work in response.

The process that this book's authors have employed—using a structured discussion protocol and gathering in virtual weekly meetings to discuss student work—is, as Christina Puntel writes in a related Digital Is resource titled "Looking with the Heart"—an "entirely remixable process" (scan the QR code or visit digitalis.nwp.org/resource/5374). In other words, educators can take what this group has done, adapt it to their own teaching needs, and engage in looking closely at student work.

The NWP's history of looking closely at student work is both long and deep. Digital Is provides a fertile environment for the continued growth, use, and active spread of this practice. Now that new ground has been broken open in digital spaces being created and used both by and outside of schools, and so much richness has taken root, NWP invites teachers to get their hands dirty, plant new seeds, and make the process of looking closely at student work—especially students' digital writing—their own. For these teachers who are ready to grow, Troy Hicks and his contributors have created an invaluable resource with which teachers can expand how they examine, appreciate, and develop their students' digital writing.

—Christina Cantrill, National Writing Project

Acknowledgments

As with any book, there are many colleagues who have contributed to my thinking, writing, researching, revising, and rewriting—so many conversations, so many presentations, so many of you to thank.

At risk of forgetting entirely too many people, please accept my sincere thanks if I have discussed this book with you at some point or another in the past few years. I thank you for asking about this project, and for listening intently as I shared our group's work.

One colleague who has taken an intense interest in this group of teachers and the ways in which we have created this book is Christina Cantrill of the National Writing Project. She and I have had so many conversations about this project, many of them happening well before I knew this was going to become a project. She has invited us to share our work at the NWP annual meeting and on the Digital Is website, and I am sure that future opportunities will continue to present themselves. Thank you, Christina, for your continued support and encouragement.

A second colleague that I must thank—as a leader in our field, as a mentor of mine, and as the writer of this book's foreword—is Richard Beach. Thank you, Rick, for the many conversations and words of encouragement you have offered me over the past decade.

Another colleague who deserves my thanks is my editor at Teachers College Press, Jean Ward. When we began conversations about this project a few years ago, it was just an elevator pitch. Over many proposal revisions and conversations, we worked together to create a vision for the collection, a vision that has finally come to fruition. For your persistence and patience, I thank you, Jean.

In that same spirit, there is an entire team at Teachers College Press who have brought this book to life, including Karl Nyberg, Nancy Power, Emily Renwick, and Dave Strauss.

A quick note of thanks to three people with whom I have shared so much of my thinking and who, in return, have been generous with their feedback—my writing group: Anne Whitney, Leah Zuidema, and Jim Fredricksen.

And, of course, I offer my sincere thanks to the teacher writers who have contributed chapters in this collection: Erin Klein, Julie Johnson, Jeremy Hyler, Bonnie Kaplan and Jack Zangerle, Christina Puntel, and Stephanie West-Puckett. Your approaches to teaching, writing, and reflecting on your work are all guided by our shared NWP principles, and I appreciate the work that you do each day with your students. You trusted me to guide you in this journey toward publication, and I am happy to share credit for this book with all of you.

Thank you.

—Troy Hicks, January 2015

Assessing Students' Digital Writing

Introduction

An Invitation to Look Closely at Students' Work

Troy Hicks

Chippewa River Writing Project (Michigan)

> What would it look like if the language of assessment was closely aligned with the language used by the creators and readers of digital compositions? It would mean that our assessment conversations would need to go far beyond what conventional rubrics and assessment programs aim to touch.
>
> —Multimodal Assessment Project (MAP) Group (2013)

Look closely.

When was the last time that you spent more than just a moment, perhaps even a few precious minutes, looking closely at one piece of student work? What can we see when we look at work together, as colleagues, and examine student work with an open mind? What might we learn from our students, from one another, and about ourselves as teachers?

As simple as it sounds, looking closely at student work presents real challenges. We often lack the time, let alone the fortitude, to examine every single piece of student work in great detail. We simply cannot afford the minutes to look at every piece of writing, every project, and every test with the same degree of care. It is often difficult to look at every piece of student work at all, let alone to examine it with the time and attention that everyone deserves. As teachers of writing like you, the contributors to this book understand this ongoing dilemma.

Perhaps one incredibly good—or incredibly bad—example of work will jump out at us while we are conferring or responding to students' assignments. Perhaps we will have the wherewithal to actually jot ourselves a note when a student says something brilliant in class discussion. And, if we are just lucky enough, we get to share one of those examples with the student and his or her parents briefly during conferences.

However, we need to be doing this more often, and with a wider variety of student work. In an age where *digital is,* we can no longer afford to look at student work in the ways we have in the past. In the compositions our students create with tools ranging from word processors to video editing suites, in genres ranging from traditional essays to podcasts, posters, and short films, "the skills and capacities  essential to new digital literacies can be directly at odds with norms and expectations that undergird most assessment programs" (NWP, DeVoss, Eidman-Aadahl, & Hicks, 2010, p. 92). This quote emerged from our book *Because Digital Writing Matters*, and more information about the book—and these new skills and capacities—can be found by scanning the QR code or visiting digitalis.nwp.org/resource/1957.

Five years on from *Because Digital Writing Matters*, the argument we present in this book, as a group of teacher researchers, boiled down to its essence, is twofold. First, we agree that looking closely at student work can yield amazing results; we know this from research as well as from our own experiences participating in many teacher inquiry groups, and especially from our work together in the process of writing. Second, we understand that both the processes and products of writing continue to undergo change in the digital age; thus, it is crucial that teachers at all grade levels begin to initiate serious conversations about how writing is taught, how we value the process of writing, and how we pay attention to the assessments of students' multimodal compositions. This introductory chapter is built around these two themes: the importance of looking closely at student work, and the necessity of changing assessment practices with and for digital writing. I examine each in turn.

LOOKING CLOSELY AT STUDENT WORK:
EMPLOYING PROTOCOLS FOR TEACHER INQUIRY

As I write the introduction to this book, state legislators and governors continue to bicker about the implementation of the Common Core State Standards (CCSS) and related assessments designed as computer-adaptive examinations for each grade level. Some states are forging ahead with the Common Core, others are pulling out their support, and a smaller number still never signed on in the first place. Fueled by the scholarship and activism of Diane Ravitch (2011, 2013), and coupled with the rising tide of the United Opt Out movement and the work of groups such as Fairtest and the Badass Teachers Association, it is interesting to note that the topic of "assessment" is actually very popular in the educational landscape at the moment.

Even a brief look at titles of educational books, journal articles, and conference presentations that have emerged in the past few years would demonstrate our increasing concerns about assessment, and for good reason. Wiggins and McTighe released the second edition of *Understanding by Design* in 2005, a book designed to differentiate between assessment and evaluation, where assessment is "the giving and using of feedback against standards to enable improvement and the meeting of goals" (2005, p. 6) was contrasted with the evaluative standardized testing requirements of the No Child Left Behind movement. Additionally, scholars such as James Popham (2008), John Hattie (2008), and Margaret Heritage (2010) have been leading advocates for formative assessment over the past decade. Unfortunately, the tide toward standardized testing still seems to be crashing against the schoolhouse doors, though individual educators—as well as teacher inquiry groups—offer teachers some shelter.

This recent shift in conversations about assessment has emerged from the No Child Left Behind era, when public discourses about what counted as "research"—and thus what could receive federal dollars for supporting programs that work—were tied to a metaphorical gold standard for research design, described on the What Works Clearinghouse (2002) page in this manner:

Study designs that provide the strongest evidence of effects include: randomized controlled trials, regression discontinuity designs, quasi-experimental designs (must use a similar comparison group and have no attrition or disruption problems), and single subject designs. For example, qualitative case studies are not in the scope of the WWC's review because they are not outcome evaluations. Therefore, a qualitative case study would not pass this screen.

In order to qualify as a valid measure of student achievement by this definition, studies needed to adhere to a model of experimental or quasi-experimental designs. Notice that qualitative case studies—the heart of teacher research—are not considered valid. It is only considered a "study" if it has a "control" and an "experimental" group, where an "intervention" is used with the experimental group. In medical studies, those in the "control" group would get a placebo. Or, in the case of education studies, teachers and students would get nothing. Measurements are taken both before and after the intervention to show if there are statistically significant differences between the experimental and control group.

To put this in human terms, what it means is that "studies"—which are actually groups of people that include the researcher, the school personnel consenting to the study and intervention taking place, the students who give their assent to being studied, and the parents who give their consent for their children to be studied—give one group of teachers and students a new textbook, instructional method, or computer program to see if they can outperform their peers who, in contrast, do not get anything new. In an effort to bring scientific validity to educational research, these controlled, randomized experiments were considered the "gold standard." While there are a number of critiques to this approach, and reading them can offer us insights into the ways that corporations lobbied hard enough to convince our congress and president that textbooks, tests, and computer programs could solve our educational woes, I will not delve deeply into that argument. Instead, my purpose here is to set up a contrast between this type of research and, on the other hand, teacher research.

Long valued as a way to look at students' work, as well as the instruction that leads to that work, *teacher research* can be defined as a systematic inquiry process conducted by teachers in their own classrooms and schools (Chiseri-Strater & Sunstein, 2006; Cochran-Smith & Lytle, 1992, 2009; Fleischer, 1995; Goswami, Lewis, Rutherford, & Waff, 2009; Goswami & Stillman, 1987; Lankshear, 2004; MacLean, Mohr, & National Writing Project (U.S.), 1999; Mohr, 2004; Stock,

1995, 2001). This type of inquiry involves the collection of particular forms of data—including samples of student work, surveys, interviews, and artifacts created by the teachers themselves—and a process of triangulation in which the teachers answer their inquiry questions by analyzing and comparing these data. In short, teacher research may not meet the "gold standard" of an empirical research design, yet there are important implications for this type of work, both practical and ethical, for the teachers who are involved in it. Cochran-Smith and Lytle (1992) explain the types of intellectual effort needed:

> Participation in teacher research requires considerable effort by innovative and dedicated teachers to stay in their classrooms and at the same time carve out opportunities to inquire and reflect on their own practice. (p. 20)

Teacher research, too, requires different perspectives about what constitutes "good" or "effective" research. Ruth Ray (1996) outlines a few differences:

> Teachers, as participants, assume the reliability of lived experience, while researchers, as observers, stand back and question it. The goals of research are different, too. Teachers conduct research because of its transformative potential for themselves and their classrooms; researchers conduct research because of its transformative potential for their fields. These differences between participant and observer are significant. Teachers are immersed in the environment; researchers, no matter how reflective and participatory, are always at some remove from it. (p. 291)

These leaders in the teacher-research movement show that, in contrast to the empirically designed, randomized studies that NCLB promoted, teachers are doing a different kind of work when they engage in inquiry. However, in a practical sense, the sad truth of the matter is that teacher researchers are still not likely to win a competitive grant from the government. The models of research proposed under NCLB continue, in a slightly different form, in the new regime's Race to the Top plan. Also, teacher research takes time, energy, and expertise that is different than what can be produced through a statistically controlled study. Teacher researchers volunteer their time to carry out this work above and beyond the typical duties associated with teaching and learning in K–12 schools.

Finally, sharing student work requires that we—all of us who teach, at all grade levels—adhere to a professional standard above and beyond what we would normally expect of one another. In an era of intense teacher evaluation, it is admirable that teacher researchers are still willing to put themselves under the microscope. This is a scary, uncomfortable place for anyone, especially many teachers who—in many states—are now being judged on a whole new set of standards related to teacher evaluation, retention, and promotion. We share our students' work, as well as our own, because we know that doing so opens us up to admitting mistakes, to showing the faults in our teaching. And, most importantly, we open up to learning, growth, and change.

It is in this spirit, one of teacher inquiry, through colleagues at the National Writing Project, that I was first introduced to "protocols" as a way to examine student work. As described by Allen and Blythe (2004), "protocols are structures that enable educators . . . to look carefully and collaboratively at student and teacher work in order to learn from it" (p. 9). Established protocols that use insightful questions give us frames for conversation, ways to guide our talking and thinking as we try to examine, not critique, students' work. Moreover, in looking at student work, groups of teachers have the potential to see more than what an individual teacher can identify on his or her own. A number of groups have developed and promoted the use of protocols, including the National Center for Restructuring Education, Schools, and Teaching at Teachers College, Columbia University; Harvard's Project Zero; and the National School Reform Faculty. As Allen and Blythe conclude, "In protocols, as in most other professional and personal endeavors, it is the questions, after all, that make real learning possible" (p. 122).

One particular protocol, the Collaborative Assessment Conference, is described by Allen and Blythe (2004) as an opportunity for teachers "to hone their ability to look closely at, articulate questions about, and interpret students' work" (p. 14). Like all protocols, the successful use of the collaborative assessment conference requires that participants engage fully and are willing to offer honest responses. It begins with the presenting teacher sharing a selected piece of student work, saying nothing at all about the work itself, the context in which it was created, or the student who created it. With traditional print-based texts, this would often involve photocopying so that each teacher researcher at the table could look closely at the student's work in his or her own hands. With digital texts, of course, we are all looking at the work on-screen.

Then, during three consecutive rounds of discussion, the facilitator would guide participants to reply to three questions: (1) "What do you see?" (2) "What questions does this work raise for you?" and (3) "What do you think this student is working on?" Participants are required to offer nonevaluative comments about the work, which can sometimes be quite difficult for us as teachers to do. Whereas our natural impulse is to find the mistake and help a student fix it, or perhaps fix it ourselves, the protocol discussion demands that we identify traits of the work without judgment. So, if a student's sentence ended without a period, the participants' observation about what they saw could not be: "This student doesn't know how to use a period." Instead, she would need to reply: "I notice that there is no punctuation mark at the end of the sentence." Again, it is often difficult for us as teachers to shift from an evaluative to a descriptive stance, mostly because of the discourse surrounding educational reforms of the past 20 years, but this is part of what the Collaborative Assessment Conference protocol forces us to do.

Moreover, while the group discusses the student's work, the presenting teacher is asked to remain silent. This, too, contradicts what we usually understand about how a professional conversation might unfold. Often, a presenter introduces an idea and asks for the audience's response; then they may dialogue about those responses and generate shared understanding. Instead, with the Collaborative Assessment Conference protocol, the presenting teacher listens carefully and takes notes, saving all comments and questions for the group until the very end. While it may feel strange at first, nearly every teacher with whom I have used this protocol shares his or her powerful reaction when we finish. Typically, they say something like this: "It was so powerful to hear others talk about my student's work in this manner. I am so glad that I had time to listen."

As we consider this process, Carini (2011) offers a few other guiding principles for describing student work:

- To treat the work seriously, not dismissively (e.g., "typical of drawings by 5-year-olds").
- To set aside the evaluation baggage of "correctness," maturity, etc.
- To view the work as active—as thought in process—recognizing that it is not definitive and, by the same token, neither is it exhaustible.

- To recognize that description lays out a range of meaning, of possibilities; that it is not intended to be an explanation or to answer the question of why the child drew it or to draw definitive conclusions.
- To let description do its work by not leaping to huge interpretations of the picture, psychological or otherwise. (p. 38)

Keeping these ideas in mind, we can begin to look without judgment. And if we look closely enough, this protocol process even has the potential to change our teaching.

Herein rests the premise of this book and our work together as a group of teacher researchers. Through a close analysis of student work, we knew that we wanted to write case studies centered on evidence we have surfaced from students' digital writing. By looking closely at individual pieces of student work, this book consists of chapters that are interwoven with two main components: (1) an analysis of a sample of a student's digital writing, and (2) a reflection on the effects that student's work had on their teaching. Taken together, this approach invites us to consider new ways of assessing students' digital writing.

CHANGING ASSESSMENT PRACTICES WITH DIGITAL WRITING

Just as we have decades of evidence from teacher research that shows the benefits of looking closely at students' work in order to better understand what they are learning, we also know that the types of work that students are producing has been changing in the past decade, largely due to the influences of newer literacies and technologies. Less well known, however, are the effects that these changes have had on assessment. As Michael Neal (2010) reminds us, the pressures on school administrators to generate usable data about student performance has led much of the conversation about writing assessment to be focused on computerized scoring of standard essays, not on creating digital compositions. He argues:

Many of the most widespread writing assessment technologies currently in use too often result in reductive, diminished views of writing and undermine our best efforts to deliver effective writing instruction and assessment. (p. 132)

Despite these challenges—including the new computerized assessments for the Common Core—many teachers, from kindergarten to graduate school, have begun a more intentional process of integrating digital writing into their curriculum and instruction. Broadly defined, *digital writing* can be any type of *"compositions created with, and oftentimes for, reading and/or viewing via a computer or other device that is connected to the Internet"* (NWP et al., 2010, p. 7; emphasis in original). Ranging from documents created with collaborative word processors to wikis, websites, podcasts, videos, or other forms of multimedia, digital writing has many proponents across professional literacy organizations such as NWP as well as the National Council of Teachers of English (NCTE) (e.g., 2007, 2013), the International Literacy Association (e.g., 2009), and the International Society for Technology in Education (ISTE) (e.g., Gura, 2014). Advocates of integrating writing instruction with other types of 21st-century literacies suggest that benefits include students' improvement with functional computer skills, as well as the ability to create web-based texts and multimodal compositions with images, sounds, and narration. Along with improving student motivation, these digital writing tasks invite more sophisticated thinking through the integration of text, spoken words, images, videos, hyperlinks, and other digital modes of expression.

As we consider what it means to teach digital writing, we owe a great deal to the 2009 NWP and Teachers College Press collection of essays, *Teaching the New Writing* (Herrington, Hodgson, & Moran, 2009). From digital picture books to collaborative editing and networks of student bloggers, this collection highlights many effective teaching practices that lead to students' production of digital writing. The stated purpose of *Teaching the New Writing* is to prompt teachers to "reflect on their own conceptions of writing-related teaching practice" (p. ix), and the book has done a wonderful job of accomplishing this goal. From Solomon's "Three Cs of Online Writing" that include "composing, computers and commotion" (p. 35), to Allison's vision of a "self-sponsored, passion-led, inquiry-based" blogging curriculum (p. 90), to Kittle's description of active student engagement in multimedia projects (p. 178), *Teaching the New Writing* gives us many thoughtful perspectives on what it means to teach digital writing, from elementary school through college.

And while the issue of assessment is woven throughout the text, it has been my experience through numerous professional development sessions and my own research that many teachers are still struggling with that issue. Assessment of digital texts, as with many kinds of student writing, remains problematic. The editors of *Teaching the New Writing* sum it up this way:

> Curricula, packaged scripts, and computer programs that focus too exclusively on teaching to a standardized test—teaching the forms of a five-paragraph print essay—are limiting students' possibilities as writers, failing to help them develop the literacy skills needed for 21st-century communication, and giving them the message that the value of their work, and, more broadly, their global competence as composers, is to be assigned by un-named strangers who may determine that more than half of them fall into the category "needs improvement." (p. 207)

As schools continue to debate the adoption of laptops, tablets, or bring-your-own-device programs, many fear that these packaged scripts, programs, and websites may offer a panacea for struggling schools, a dream too good to be true. Rather than teaching digital writing in thoughtful, productive, and critical ways, teachers in this era run the risk of adopting (or being forced to adopt) poor practices for teaching digital writing that lead to even worse outcomes for students as writers overall, in both print and nonprint contexts. Because the shift in focus on students' performance will become even more acute when we are faced with yearly tests under the Common Core plan, now is the time to think carefully about how students' digital work can inform our instruction and assessment.

Moreover, despite the enthusiasm that teaching digital writing has created, little systematic evidence exists that supports the contention that these approaches and assignments actually improve student writing performance or teachers' abilities to assess that performance in substantive ways. In some ways, this is a solution looking for a problem; must we assess everything that students do in school? In others, however, we want to show that digital writing does, indeed, matter. Evidence does show that well-planned and executed professional development and classroom integration of one-to-one programs can show demonstrable effects in students' performance (Warschauer, 2011). Many of the web-based services (such as Google Docs, Wikispaces, and Voicethread) can be accessed on phone, tablet, or laptop/desktop PCs, making them more ubiquitous and utilitarian, and opportunities for digital writing are much more available. So, on the one hand, the challenge of lacking clear, quantifiable data about the effects of digital writing can be seen as an advantage. In other words, digital writing does not yield itself to the types of conventional assignments and assessments that we have become accustomed to in an age of standardized testing, even as it is becoming more prevalent in professional development and instruction.

On the other hand, this lack of empirical evidence related to the connections between digital writing tasks (not just computer integration in general) and student performance—either large-scale statistical samples or rich case studies—allows critics of technology to discount the possibilities of what teachers and students can accomplish. These critics claim that young people wallow in a world of viral videos, narcissistic status updates, and the latest Internet memes. Worse yet, issues such as cyberbullying have made national news as too many young people take their lives in an effort to escape harassment via text messages and social network posts. These are, indeed, real and substantive issues that should influence our conversations about how to integrate technology into our classrooms and communities.

While some of this criticism is valid—and we certainly do need to think more carefully about how to create and protect productive, ethical, and responsible digital citizens—there are also countless examples of teachers and students doing meaningful work with digital writing, work that extends our understanding of both the content of writing instruction and also the context in which students compose writing. Although not every student's work will be welcomed by a global audience simply because it has been created online and shared via class website, the fact is that students do produce better writing when the potential for an audience is present.

Taken from another angle, there is more than just digital citizenship at stake. Curriculum and assessment matter a great deal, and there are many issues left to be decided in the implementation of the Common Core State Standards, not the least of which is how phrases such as this—"Use technology, including the Internet, to produce and publish writing and present the relationships between information and ideas clearly and efficiently" (CCSS.ELA-LITERACY.W.6.6, see www.corestandards.org/ELA-Literacy/WHST/6-8/)—will be implemented in actual instructional practice. Even though the writing portion of the test will be administered on computer, that does not necessarily mean that students will be producing *digital writing*; will they have the opportunity to research and cite online sources, include hyperlinks, or compose multimedia? Likely not. So, even though the tests are administered via computer, they could still produce the kinds of formulaic writing that we have long tried to eliminate through strong writing instruction (Graham & Perin, 2007; National Writing Project & Nagin, 2006).

How we determine the worth of the work that students do, and the effects that such work has on our teaching, will matter even more than simply implementing a new curriculum. As Dohn explains, there are a number of tensions evident between traditional educational practices and the ethos of Web 2.0 activities that are founded on openness, collaboration, reuse, and a lack of finality (Dohn, 2009). Contrasted with the often closed, individual, carefully documented, final draft of a paper, integrating digital writing tools is more than just a matter of taking current school assignments and putting them online. Put another way, Knobel and Lankshear (2006) describe a shift toward a "new literacy" mindset, a mindset that places value on new ways of producing knowledge in collaboration rather than valuing isolated knowledge. It is heartening that we are, indeed, starting to see evidence of that shift in the ways that educators describe assessment practices for digital writing.

Recent innovations in assessment, such as the National Writing Project's Multimodal Assessment Project (MAP), have shown the increasing complexity of analyzing and evaluating student work produced as digital writing. Also, the field of computers and composition is broadly interested in this topic, as the March 2014 themed issue *Multimodal Assessment* of *Computers and Composition*, edited by Carl Whithaus (2014), and the recent collection *Digital Writing Assessment and Evaluation*, edited by Heidi McKee and Danielle DeVoss (2013), have demonstrated. McKee and DeVoss begin their collection by asking many questions, including this one:

> How do different approaches to assessing traditional writing (8 1/2" x 11" word-centric texts) port—or not—to the assessment of digital writing? What challenges and opportunities for assessment do multimodal, networked texts present? (Preface, para. 1)

These are significant questions because they involve both technical capacity and a new mindset toward teaching and learning writing. They are questions that we will work to answer throughout this book as we use heuristics such as the NWP's Multimodal Assessment Project (MAP Group, 2013) and the habits of mind from the Framework for Success in Postsecondary Writing (Council of Writing Program Administrators [CWPA], NCTE, & NWP, 2011). I quote extensively from these two documents in Figures I.1 and I.2 to provide readers with a sense of each and with a reference as they read the individual chapters. Moreover, I will return to both of these heuristics in the Conclusion of this book, using them to frame the discussion about where the assessment of digital writing in K–12 classrooms might go next. (Note that the "habits of mind" from the Framework for Success are similar to, but should not be confused with, the "habits of mind" developed by Art Costa and Bena Kallick [2000].)

A final framework that we introduce into this discussion is that of Connected Learning. Described by the Connected Learning Research Network scholars as "a framework for understanding and supporting learning, as well as a theory of intervention that grows out of our analysis of today's changing social, economic, technological, and cultural context" (Ito et al., 2013, p. 7), the Connected Learning Framework offers us another opportunity for thinking about how to view the work of these digital writers. Connected Learning describes three contextual conditions (learning that is peer-supported, interest-powered, and academically oriented), three experiential properties (learning is production-centered, with shared purpose, and openly networked), and a number of ways to make connected learning environments and support learning with new media. Taken as a whole, the Connected Learning framework promotes a student-centered, action-oriented model of learning that takes place, most often, in spaces outside of school. And while most of the projects that we describe in this book were created "for school," the touch points of Connected Learning will become evident.

A BRIEF DESCRIPTION OF
OUR TEACHER INQUIRY GROUP'S PROCESS

The process of writing this book has been a collaborative, collegial experience for all of us involved. I had been in conversation with Jean Ward of Teachers College Press for nearly 2 years trying to bring a proposal to fruition, building on the idea of using the Collaborative Assessment Conference (CAC) protocol to look closely at students' digital work in a way similar to what we had experienced at the NWP Digital Is conference. After a series of false starts, Jean and I met in

Figure I.1. Components from NWP's Multimodal Assessment Project

The **artifact** is the finished product. Audiences expect artifacts to convey a coherent message with a clear focus created through an appropriate use of structure, medium, and technique. Artifacts incorporate elements from multiple modes, and are often digital, but do not have to be—they may be analog works (e.g., texts that incorporate both writing and drawing). They identify the connections among resources, composers, and ideas and may demonstrate habits of mind such as innovation, creativity, and critical stance.

Context is the world around the artifact, around the creation of the artifact, and how the artifact enters, circulates, and fits into the world. Authors attend to the context of a multimodal artifact when they make design decisions related to genre or to an artifact's intended uses. Given their purposes, authors consider the affordances, constraints, and opportunities, given purpose, audience, composing environment, and delivery mode.

As a domain, **substance** refers to the content and overall quality and significance of the ideas presented. The substance of a piece is related to an artifact's message in relationship to the contextual elements of purpose, genre, and audiences. Considering the substance of a piece encourages authors to think about elements such as quality of ideas, quality of performance, credibility, accuracy, and significance.

Process management and technique refer to the skills, capacities, and processes involved in planning, creating, and circulating multimodal artifacts. Creating multimodal products involves the technical skills of production using the chosen tools, but it also includes larger project management skills as well as the ability to collaborate with others in diverse and often interactive situations. Over time, individuals learn to more effectively control the skills and manage the processes of producing and circulating digital content.

Habits of mind are patterns of behavior or attitudes that reach beyond the artifact being created at the moment. They develop over time and can be nurtured through self-sponsored learning as well as teacher-facilitated activities throughout the process. Examples include creativity, persistence, risk-taking, mindfulness, and engagement. Habits of mind can also include an openness to participatory and interactive forms of engagement with audiences.

Source: Excerpted from "Developing domains for multimodal writing assessment: The language of evaluation, the language of instruction," by NWP MAP Group, 2013, in H. A. McKee & D. N. DeVoss (Eds.), *Digital writing assessment & evaluation*. Available at ccdigitalpress.org/dwae/07_nwp.html. Reprinted with permission.

Figure I.2. Components from the Framework for Success in Postsecondary Writing

Habits **of mind** refers to ways of approaching learning that are both intellectual and practical and that will support students' success in a variety of fields and disciplines. The Framework identifies eight habits of mind essential for success in college writing:

- Curiosity—the desire to know more about the world.
- Openness—the willingness to consider new ways of being and thinking in the world.
- Engagement—a sense of investment and involvement in learning.
- Creativity—the ability to use novel approaches for generating, investigating, and representing ideas.
- Persistence—the ability to sustain interest in and attention to short- and long-term projects.
- Responsibility—the ability to take ownership of one's actions and understand the consequences of those actions for oneself and others.
- Flexibility—the ability to adapt to situations, expectations, or demands.
- Metacognition—the ability to reflect on one's own thinking as well as on the individual and cultural processes used to structure knowledge.

The Framework then explains how teachers can foster these habits of mind through **writing, reading, and critical analysis** experiences. These experiences aim to develop students'

- Rhetorical knowledge—the ability to analyze and act on understandings of audiences, purposes, and contexts in creating and comprehending texts.
- Critical thinking—the ability to analyze a situation or text and make thoughtful decisions based on that analysis, through writing, reading, and research.
- Writing processes—multiple strategies to approach and undertake writing and research.
- Knowledge of conventions—the formal rules and informal guidelines that define what is considered to be correct (or appropriate) and incorrect (or inappropriate) in a piece of writing.
- Abilities to compose in multiple environments—from using traditional pen and paper to electronic technologies.

Source: Excerpted from "Framework for success in postsecondary writing," by Council of Writing Program Administrators, NCTE, & NWP, 2011, pp. 4–10. Available at wpacouncil.org/framework.

April 2013, and in May I sent out an email invitation to potential contributors that included the book proposal, a schedule of Sunday-night Google hangouts, and a sincere request to work with a group of National Writing Project colleagues. From there, with the ball rolling, our teacher inquiry group began to meet on a regular basis for 8 weeks over the summer, and the book began to evolve.

A typical Sunday-night Google hangout would actually start a few days ahead of time, when the presenting teacher would share his or her student work as a link via email. As you will see from the variety of work outlined in the next section, we chose to view the work ahead of time—rather than during the protocol itself—because each piece required various time commitments, allowing for multiple viewings of videos, and, in the case of Christina's students' video game, for our intense desire to continue playing and beat the next level. When we would log on to the Google hangout at 8:00 on Sunday evening, we would jump right into the protocol discussion using a slightly modified version of the questions used at the NWP Digital Is conference:

- What do you see/notice?
- What is working in this piece/composition?
- What does it make you wonder/what questions does it raise?

During three rounds—one round per question—I would take notes in a Google Doc as the presenting teacher also listened to others and silently took notes. This three-round process could take anywhere from 30 to 60 minutes, depending on the composition and who was available to meet. Due to scheduling, some of us had to miss a session or two, yet most Sundays the majority of us were present to participate in the protocol discussion.

After hearing from the presenting teacher about his or her reaction to the things we noticed, what was working for us, and what questions it raised, we had a large-group discussion about possible implications. This then led to a final 5-minute freewrite where we each took time to reflect on the protocol. Over the course of the summer—and six separate protocols—each night's conversation averaged about 2,000 to 3,000 words from notes and freewrites for each teacher, thus creating the raw material for the chapters in this book.

Taken in sum, the protocol process was, as we expected, a very fruitful one for us as teachers interested in digital writing. We were able to generate a number of ideas about one piece of student work—thus allowing us to "look closely" at it—and also hear from one another about different approaches to teaching digital writing from elementary school to 1st-year college composition. Through these conversations, we developed our professional relationships and strengthened our own abilities as teachers. And now we share what we have learned with you.

OUTLINE OF THE BOOK

In this book we will look closely at a variety of student work presented by the following six teachers:

- Erin Klein, a 2nd-grade teacher at Cranbrook Schools in Bloomfield Hills, MI (Eastern Michigan Writing Project). Erin documents the process that one student, Aaron, went through to transform a print-based report on monkeys into two pieces of digital writing, using both an augmented reality application, Aurasma, and the website Smore, which allows users to make online posters.
- Julie Johnson, a 4th-grade teacher at Hilliard City Schools in Hilliard, OH (Columbus Area Writing Project). Julie introduces us to one of her students, Carson, and demonstrates how he transferred informational text about the Earth's layers into a website modeled on the Wonderopolis website.
- Jeremy Hyler, a 7th/8th-grade teacher at Fulton Schools in Fulton, MI (Chippewa River Writing Project). Jeremy describes how he modified a traditional book response into a project that required a persuasive book review as well as a short video production for a digital book trailer. He shares the work of his student Lauren.
- Bonnie Kaplan, an educational consultant and a co-director of the Hudson Valley Writing Project (New Paltz, NY); and Jack Zangerle, a middle school teacher at Dover Union Free School District (Hudson Valley Writing Project). Bonnie and Jack have collaborated on a variety of technology-rich projects, including the Public Service Announcement video created by Katie that is featured in this collection.

- Christina Puntel, a high school teacher at Philadelphia
  Schools (Philadelphia Writing Project). Christina chose a
  video game produced by students Brandon and Tre for a
  teach-in as a part of her social justice and multicultural ethics
  course.
- Stephanie West-Puckett, a teaching instructor at East Carolina
  University in Greenville, NC (Tar River Writing Project). Steph
  chose an example of a digital essay from her student Zeke,
  who created the work in the form of stop-motion animation
  for a freshman composition course.

In each chapter, we begin—as we would in the protocol discussion—with the student work itself. We invite you to view all the projects on NWP's Digital Is website by scanning the QR code or visiting digitalis.nwp.org/node/6288. Each chapter will consist of four components. First comes a description of the teaching context, followed by, second, a rich but succinct description of the writing  assignment, including the specific digital writing objective. This will help provide a bit of context for the work (although strict adherence to the CAC protocol requires the presenting teacher to avoid providing any context). Third, a summary and analysis of our group's discussion about the student's work, based on the notes taken by the presenting teacher, are provided. Finally, each chapter will conclude with a section where each author will discuss the implications for instruction and assessment.

This was time-consuming work, beginning with conversations in our inquiry group, selecting student work, meeting for hours to discuss the pieces of student work, and then drafting, revising, and editing the subsequent chapters in this book. Additionally, because the work spread out over the course of about 18 months, teachers participating in our inquiry group were able to take back the rich set of ideas and critical questions into their classroom after our initial summer conversations. Moreover, they were able to provide one another with peer reviews during the second summer, thus drawing broader thematic connections between their own chapters and the rest of the manuscript.

In the final chapter, I discuss a number of broad themes and issues about curriculum, instruction, and assessment that we have gleaned from our shared experience of studying student work. Rather than looking at broad disconnected standards or thinking specifically about one or another type of technology, in this final chapter we position ourselves as teaching leaders who want to advocate for particular kinds of principles regarding digital writing that cut across grade-level and disciplinary boundaries.

Throughout the book, we share our experiences through the voices of teachers speaking one to another, opening the conversation to you.

By doing so, we invite you to look closely, too.

CHAPTER 1

Extending Writing Through Augmented Reality

Erin Klein
Eastern Michigan Writing Project

digitalis.nwp.org/resource/6279

Working with young children is something I feel very fortunate to be able to do each day. The best part of my day is being able to share great stories with my students. They love when they see me walk in with a large plain brown bag. They know it is filled with new treasures from the local independent bookstore.

My 2nd-graders not only love the rich stories we share together, they become inspired by the authors who touch their lives. We share a strong sense of family in our classroom. We spend the first few weeks of school building routines, setting expectations, and getting to know one another. Throughout the year, we continue to do team-building activities and share our lives with one another. We have a daily show-and-tell, and I eat lunch with students every day. We are very close. When it's time for writing workshop, my students open up and share. No one is afraid to take risks. They see failure as an opportunity to improve. They incorporate such rich craft into their stories and revise several drafts before publishing a piece. Most students even come back to published pieces to revise details they have the urge to make better. I only wish I could take credit for their drive and creativity.

Our school has been using the writing units of study created by a team within our district. These units, along with our classroom culture, have enabled our young writers to support one another and believe in themselves as authors. Wanting to give these children a broader voice, I started incorporating technology into our writing workshop. The results were impressive.

CONTEXT FOR THE PROJECT

Integrating technology into the curriculum has been an evolutionary process in my teaching practice. This process really began a few years ago when I taught middle school. I started by assigning traditional projects and allowing for new ways to publish. For example, I began by having students read a book chapter and then share their thinking in a blog post rather than a composition notebook. After reflecting, I realized that I wasn't changing the cognitive task at all. Were students supposed to be inspired just because I was allowing them to type rather than print? I even tried convincing myself that students now had a global audience. This authentic and global audience would certainly be inspiring to a student. However, the sparkle of blogging soon wore off when students began to complain that no one was visiting their blogs or responding. Some even asked to go back to responding in their composition notebooks because they were faster at writing than typing. I began to wonder if I was failing my students or if it was the technology. Could it be the way I was using the technology?

Though some of my students found success with blogging, it wasn't for everyone in my class. I knew I had to offer a menu of options to my students. I couldn't tell them they all had to blog and expect them to love doing it. I needed to offer a few choices. The evolutionary process of technology integration continued. I introduced my students to a few publishing platforms and let them select which direction to take their project. For example, some students were allowed to create a digital story using Storybird (storybird.com), while others could make a multimedia poster using Glogster (edu.glogster.com). This was much more successful than having every student blog.

Even though I was providing my students with options, there was still a need for change. I couldn't simply give them a choice of media to use. Though offering the students a variety of publishing platforms, I needed to allow for more autonomy. I had to change the task. In fact, I needed to eliminate the idea of an assigned task and begin to tap into the students' vision for publishing and sharing their work. I had to learn that for each student, that approach may look different. I struggled with the idea of letting go. How much would I hold onto in order to still feel like I was teaching? I wanted to find meaningful ways to integrate technology that allowed for differentiation and choice.

After a few years of teaching middle school, I began working with 2nd-graders. Just as I was learning how to let go and allow for autonomy, I now felt as though I needed to provide these younger learners with so much more structure and explicit instruction. I had nearly forgotten what it was like when I used to teach 1st-graders years ago. However, I quickly adapted to the ever-imaginative, answer-seeking, creative, and inquisitive minds of 7- and 8-year-olds. These students weren't doing work for grades and percentages. We didn't even offer grades at the 2nd-grade level. Instead, these students were doing work in order to achieve their personal best efforts. They asked more questions, did more revisions, and took greater risks. Part of me wondered if I was inhibiting my former middle schoolers by giving grades.

My 2nd-graders were far more independent and creative than I had anticipated. I expected them to be vastly different from my former middle school students; however, I found that they were actually quite similar. My class of 7- and 8-year-olds were curious, technology-savvy learners. They were ready for choice and challenge.

Our class began using technology and publishing digitally. At the end of each day, we did digital workstations. As I worked with small groups at one workstation, other students in partnerships would rotate through two different stations. Sometimes one station featured playing a math game on ABCya.com, while the other station had students create a digital story using an application like Toontastic on the iPad. Each week the stations would change. Over time, the children learned to use a variety of web tools, applications, and devices. These digital workstations not only allowed time for me to meet with small groups of students but also enabled my students to become proficient and confident using technology as a tool for learning and sharing.

One of my students' favorite applications to use was Aurasma (aurasma.com). Aurasma is a free application that allows users to create augmented reality. Augmented reality allows someone to add another layer to an existing image. For example, imagine holding your phone over a poster on the wall as if you were going to take a photo of that poster, and then instantly a video starts playing to offer you additional information about that particular poster. I began using augmented reality to extend my students' learning. We started with making our word walls come to life. Because I only have one school-issued iPad, I also used my personal iPad and iPhone. I borrowed my colleague's school iPad and iPhone, too. This gave us 5 devices to use. We had to share, but it was manageable and didn't take much time.

During one lesson on weight and capacity, I had my students think of a brief way to describe each vocabulary term in the lesson. I simply passed out index cards and had each child work with a partner. They chose a word to define or explain and then came up with a brief explanation or example of the term. One partner took a short video of the other partner explaining the vocabulary word. They wrote the word on the index card. This index card became their trigger image. Next, they opened the Aurasma app, snapped a photo of the index card, and selected the video they took from their camera roll to be applied as the overlay. When each partnership finished, they put tape on their index card and stuck it to our math word wall (in our room, this is just a sheet of chart paper on the wall). We keep an iPad nearby. Now, when anyone wishes to hear more about any specific vocabulary term, they can hover the iPad (or iPhone) above the word on the word wall. The student-created video overlay will automatically begin playing.

The students loved this activity. Seeing their words come to life was such an inspiration. The class has asked to make future words augmented. Since I've already taught the process, I allow them to do this independently. This has become an extension they can work on when they finish early or have something additional to add to a lesson. It's empowering! This one simple task has encouraged all of my learners to dig deeper into the meanings of words and think creatively about their work. They love the idea that this activity is authentic and that anyone can view their Aura. It has encouraged students to take ownership of their learning and to produce quality work in a meaningful way.

DESCRIBING THE PROJECT

Each year all 2nd-grade students get to select their own animal to research and then write a report based on that research. This research unit focuses on two Common Core Writing Standards:

#2: Write informative/explanatory texts in which they introduce a topic, use facts and definitions to develop points, and provide a concluding statement or section.

#7: Participate in shared research and writing projects (e.g., read a number of books on a single topic to produce a report; record science observations). (www.corestandards.org/ELA-Literacy/W/2/)

As a class, we first study several authors and a variety of mentor texts, thinking carefully about what needs to go into the process of writing an informational text. This provides us with a framework of what to expect from this genre of writing. Many of the students can easily identify the differences between fiction and nonfiction. However, in an effort to prepare students to write in this genre, a structure must be introduced and students must possess knowledge about the topic.

The following questions guide our lessons.

- How do writers learn from mentor text the qualities of effective informational text?
- How do writers access and confirm prior knowledge of a topic?
- How do writers do research to gather and record information?
- How do writers plan and draft information in an organized way?
- How do writers read and revise using strategies to increase the amount and quality of information given?
- How do writers prepare for publication by checking spelling and punctuation before sharing their work with others?
- How do writers share their work with others?

During a 2-week time frame students are immersed in mentor texts and begin conducting their research on their animal. As the 3rd week approaches, many of the students begin to draft their reports. They focus their research on three main components: animal habitat, diet, and physical characteristics. Students take notes, draft their research, revise their work, design their page layouts, and publish their work. Because students are working at their own pace, some require more assistance and some finish before others. When I observe the amount of work that the children put into their research and writing, I wonder how I can make their process more meaningful. I find myself reflecting on the last essential question that guides our lessons: How do writers share their work with others?

During writing workshop, students often have several creative ideas for publishing their work using a digital platform since they've grown so used to using digital tools. As some students began to finish their work, I knew I had to develop some extension activities to keep those learners involved and engaged. Before I could properly create and plan for these meaningful and standards-aligned extension activities, one student took me by surprise when he finished before some of the other students whom I knew were wrapping up their reports.

Aaron, my early finisher, was so proud of his written report on monkeys (Figure 1.1 shows the cover). He couldn't wait to show it off and share with others what he had researched. He asked if he could augment his report. This also took me by surprise. While we had used augmented reality in our room, I had never had a student apply his or her learning to a project using such technology. I didn't know what guidelines to give him in that precise moment. Yet I could see the excitement in his face and anticipation in his eyes, waiting for me to give him permission to move forward with his idea. Who was I to not allow him to creatively publish his work? After all, he had already completed the assigned portion of the project. Besides, I had some students who weren't as far along and really needed some support to revise their work. I decided to allow Aaron to work independently and create his augmented project.

As I was working with other students, I noticed Aaron gathering chart paper and markers. He walked over to an open space in our reading area and began spreading out his materials for his work space. With no direction, this student was taking complete ownership of his learning. I was bubbling with anticipation to see what he would produce. When our workshop time ended for the day, students were asked to clean up and gather for our closing share time. Aaron asked if he'd be allowed to continue his work tomorrow. Aaron was typically the type of student who likes to get projects and assignments checked off his list. I was delighted to hear him ask if he could continue working the next day.

Aaron continued to work over the next few days. I saw him illustrating a poster on large chart paper, rereading his animal report, going back to the books he used for research to reference more about

Figure 1.1. Aaron's Initial Report on Monkeys

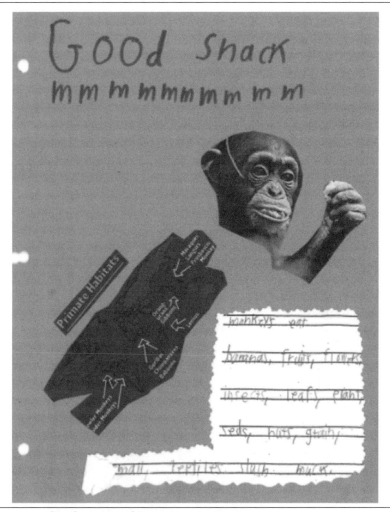

Image reproduced courtesy of Smore/www.smore.com.

monkeys, sketching out a storyboard of his commercial plan, and rehearsing his lines for the camera. Though I didn't know exactly what he was planning, I was able to piece some of his ideas together by seeing his detailed planning. He was taking his own project very seriously. When he was finally finished, he asked if I'd like to see what he had been working to complete. Aaron handed me an iPad and asked that I hold it over the chart paper he illustrated.

LOOKING CLOSELY AT AARON'S WORK

I walked over to the colorfully illustrated chart paper he had hung on the wall (see Figure 1.2). When I got closer, I could see a slight grin begin to emerge from his face. I began reading his poster. I first noticed his creative choice in color. Aaron had decided to use alternating orange, green, yellow, and blue colors to display the text on his poster. I could tell he took his time, and his work showed that he carefully crafted his sentences. After reading his poster advertisement for visiting the monkey exhibit at the zoo, I held the iPad in front of the paper. I pushed the iPad's home button, swiped to find the Aurasma application, tapped it to open the selected app, and held the iPad very still, hovering over his poster. As soon as I did, the video he had created

Figure 1.2. A Screenshot from Aaron's Aurasma Video

began to play. He had set his chart paper poster to be the trigger image that would allow his video to begin playing. The video segment was in the style of a commercial.

Aaron's video immediately came on the iPad screen and he introduced himself as a zookeeper for the Detroit Zoo. I appreciated his creativity to transform his narrative into a persuasive monologue where he really pulled his audience in by taking on the role of zookeeper. Aaron called on information he had displayed on his poster while explaining how monkeys are different from one another. Next, he showed diversity in the zoo's monkeys by telling his audience, "Four new monkeys just arrived!" Aaron talked about their sizes and names. Aaron proceeded to give some information about the monkeys and even suggested that visitors bring a water bottle for the hot day. He directed his remarks to the audience as an official zookeeper. When the video was over, I glanced over at Aaron and saw his beaming face. He was grinning so hard I could tell he was proud of the work he had done. Now anyone subscribed to our class channel could look at his poster with the Aurasma app and play his commercial video.

I could tell that Aaron really grew as a writer with this project in several ways. Aaron typically completes his writing early on in the process. He often needs encouragement to go back and revise his work or extend his thinking. However, with this project Aaron was taking ownership of his learning and extending his own thinking. Without being continually prompted, he was taking the initiative to highlight his creativity in various writing media. Upon reflection, I would like to have seen Aaron go back and do the same level of revision with his video as he did with his writing. I believe that level of revision would have made his work that much stronger. He did a superb job including voice in his narrative and carrying that over into his multimedia project, too. I would encourage him, in the future, to go through the peer revision process to receive feedback and make improvements as he plays with this sort of media again.

I could clearly see Aaron's understanding of the genre of advertising, even though we had not studied this genre in class. The promotional nature of the video, coupled with his enthusiasm and sense of urgency, spoke to the dynamic and powerful project he developed. Aaron had made connected meaning across texts. His choice in selecting a video platform to publish allowed his audience to hear his voice. Aaron's audience could see his passion, knowledge, and understanding through his written book, artistically created poster, and interactive video.

So now that Aaron had published his report using augmented reality, he asked if he could continue working with technology to publish his research in another medium. One of the digital tools the students have used in the past was Smore (smore.com), a web tool that allows users to import text and media to create a digital poster online. Because I was still conferring with other groups of students, I allowed Aaron to extend his project into the digital realm. While not all of my students could have completed this task independently, Aaron possessed the prerequisite skills needed for this project. For example, he knew how to safely search for images online, save them to a folder, and upload them within a given platform. I simply had to log him into my account so that he could begin creating.

Smore is a platform for creating digital posters that look professional yet are rather simple to put together. I enjoy this web tool because the students gain basic knowledge of navigating simple computer functionality like saving and uploading, but they can also focus more on the content rather than the bells and whistles of the platform. Because of Smore's simple-to-use interface, users can easily select from a variety of predesigned layouts. Once users have decided on a design theme, or layout, they can begin adding their information. The user has creative freedom in color choice, design layout, font selection, written content, and visual aides, or images.

One key factor I noticed as I conferred with students in my class was that Aaron was not just designing a digital poster, he was also furthering his research. He wasn't working to change his font size and color multiple times. Instead, he had several tabs open across the top of the screen. I noticed him navigating between sites he had opened from our school's library page of secure resources. Whether or not he was going to add this new information to his digital poster, he was certainly expanding his knowledge. As he began to upload his information, I saw him walk around the room to collect a variety of different mentor texts we had used during lessons. Curious, I paused to observe his intentions with these books. As I stood in the back of the classroom with a group of writers who were revising their written work, I could see that Aaron was using the mentor texts as guides for his digital poster layout. He was taking notice of headings, fonts, captions, and many more nonfiction text features. Not only was he furthering his research, utilizing web tools, and studying mentor texts, he was also paying close attention to the structure and features within the text.

I was able to gather the following from Aaron's Smore poster:

- He uses different fonts and font sizes for different parts of the poster.
- His subheadings take on a first-person narrative as if he were the monkey, allowing for his creative license.
- The images highlight three types of monkeys.
- Each title of the picture and the caption correlate.
- Aaron explicitly points out that not all monkeys are alike by showing the reader the different colors in the pictures and writing about their varying size.
- He knows how to use commas to separate words in a series.

It was clear to me that when I agreed to join this team of authors and embark on the journey through completing the Collaborative Assessment Protocol, Aaron's work would be the artifact to evaluate and examine. I chose Aaron's work for a variety of reasons. First, I always like to highlight young boy writers. I believe there is a negative stereotype placing a stigma on developing male writers. Therefore, I am sure to always highlight boy writing in the workshops I host and through the artifacts I share. Another reason I selected Aaron's work is because, as previously mentioned, he often rushed through his work in an effort to have the assignment completed. This was a turning point for his writing process. Though he still exhibited a tendency to finish quickly, he was beginning to understand the meaning of writing as a process. Aaron had been set in having each task he started being completed that day. It was a challenge for him to leave a project unfinished. Additionally, if you asked him to revisit the same project on a different day, he was reluctant to do so (for that project was already completed). However, his interest and engagement in this project seemed to change his perspective. Finally, I chose Aaron's work for this process because of his passion for the work he was doing. His excitement for sharing his digitally published work was becoming contagious in our classroom. His journey was a story I knew needed to be told.

IMPLICATIONS FOR INSTRUCTION AND ASSESSMENT

Aaron's example of augmented reality and his digital Smore poster were unique in that they were not a planned project intended for assessment. Traditionally, I like to plan with my students and decide the essential learning objectives for the unit and how we will accomplish those objectives. As a class, we determine how we will demonstrate our understanding. For example, when we knew we had to show proficiency in understanding text features, the class decided we should study various nonfiction texts to compare and contrast our observations. Then we determined that we could create our own nonfiction book as an artifact that demonstrated our knowledge and understanding. However, once Aaron met those objectives, he thought of a creative way to extend his thinking. I had not prepared lessons to scaffold his learning, nor did I give him rubrics ahead of time. Yet I decided it was best to keep him working within the unit of study—nonfiction—so I gave him permission to work independently.

Looking back, I am proud of the work Aaron did, but I can see some areas where I could have supported his efforts in a more intentional manner.

In writing workshop I don't usually have extension activities available for students. We follow the mantra made popular by Lucy Calkins in her books and presentations: "When you're done, you've only just begun." In our class, students are encouraged to add more detail to their work or are asked to start another piece. However, seeing Aaron's level of engagement and writing stamina increase, I have been thinking about how to provide more opportunities for students to publish digitally.

When evaluating student work, I use a proficiency checklist along with a student reflection questionnaire to determine whether or not the learner has met the standard(s) being assessed. I also use the proficiency checklist to guide my writing lessons and conferences with the class and with small groups or individuals. According to the proficiency checklists our district used, publishing digitally wouldn't change the assessment process. Therefore, it is my goal to start introducing the students to more tools that would allow them to share their work in more creative ways.

After going through this process, I have realized the importance of finding balance in allowing students to have autonomy yet still providing them with the necessary tools and guidance. While Aaron was able to take on such tasks independently, not all of my students would be able to do so. Additionally, even though Aaron did publish his work digitally, I wonder how it could have been enhanced with a bit of mentoring and support. I think the augmented reality project and publishing the digital Smore poster were beneficial extensions that naturally fit into Aaron's work. Upon reflecting, I would have liked to encourage him to take his new research and find ways to integrate it into his written work as well. I think the details he could have added would have enhanced his nonfiction piece and enabled his readers to learn a great deal more about his animal. Lastly, I believe that having such opportunities would allow all students to benefit, not just those who finish early. Allowing students to express their work as they see it allows their voices to not only be heard but also seen. Technology can be a tool that enables the student voice to more accurately be expressed in a creative outlet.

CHAPTER 2

Wondering in Room 114

Julie Johnson
Columbus Area Writing Project (Ohio)

digitalis.nwp.org/resource/6280

In my classroom, we wonder. We wonder how wildfires start. We wonder what is the largest dog in the world. We wonder who invented Legos. My 4th-graders are full of questions. Their curiosity is contagious.

We set the stage for wondering from the very beginning of the school year. Inquiry is the foundation on which I build my curriculum. My 4th-grade students know that our classroom is safe; it is a place to ask questions, take risks, make mistakes, and learn. I want my students to take ownership of their learning and to produce work that is both meaningful and purposeful to them. I provide spaces and time for those very important conversations that grow student learning. Books, both fiction and nonfiction, line the walls in my classroom. Websites are posted so that students can read articles and blogs online.

Of course, we know the importance of inquiry as adults. When I encounter a new topic, I approach my reading and writing as a novice, and I find many opportunities for wonder. I might want to research interesting places to visit on vacation or learn more about a new topic I am teaching. I may be wondering how to create healthier meals for my family or where to find more information on ridding my garden of pests. When searching for answers to my wonders, I begin with a sense of curiosity and purpose. I jot questions down on paper and gather resources. I read books, blogs, and websites. I ask for advice from other people who have more knowledge on the subject than I do. As I go through this process, I sift through the plethora of information to determine what is pertinent to what I need to know. My reading life revolves around being able to synthesize, analyze, and evaluate informational texts.

This knowledge about myself as a learner validates my beliefs as a teacher. Christopher Lehman (2012) tells us,

> Teaching students to research, then, does not begin by assigning finite topics and handing out pre-selected sources. Instead, it begins by embracing the uncertainty all of us feel when first researching a topic, then teaching budding researchers to do the things we have learned to do. (p. 9)

I want my students to experience reading and writing in this authentic, purposeful environment.

Though you and I can make these moves as adults, we need to be intentional when structuring an inquiry stance for our students. Katie Wood Ray (1999) tells us about the importance of reading with the lens of a craft person, like a seamstress studies the handiwork of clothes. Taking the time to read and study digital writing becomes an integral piece of my language arts block.

Additionally, the introduction to the CCSS states that students who meet the standards do these things:

> habitually perform the critical reading necessary to pick carefully through the staggering amount of information available today *in print and digitally.* They actively seek the wide, deep, and thoughtful engagement with high-quality literary and informational texts that builds knowledge, enlarges experience, and broadens worldviews. (www.corestandards.org/assets/CCSSI_ELA%20Standards.pdf, p. 3, emphasis added)

Therefore, learning how to navigate informational text, both in print and online, becomes integral to my teaching. With the new emphasis on close reading from the CCSS, it becomes even more important to teach students how to read and write texts with the purpose of gaining a deeper understanding of the key details, author's message, and text structure. In addition, students need to be able to interpret information that is presented visually (charts, graphs, timelines, and so on) and explain how the information contributes to the understanding of the text in which it appears (www.corestandards.org/ELA-Literacy/RI/4/7/).

Given these standards, my teaching must take an inquiry-based approach. So we ask questions and seek out new ideas. Carson, like all of my students, was wondering, too. Through the process of looking closely at Carson's Wonder project, I discuss how I set up the writing workshop in my classroom, which includes incorporating digital mentor texts, using Wonderopolis (wonderopolis.org), and focusing on digital, critical, and visual literacies. Next, I introduce how our teacher inquiry group's use of the protocol discussion led me to new understandings of Carson's project. Here, I dig deeply into his work and the decisions he made as a digital composer. I then end by sharing my reflections on the process.

OUR WRITING WORKSHOP

According to Donald Graves, a strong workshop has the following four components: time, choice in topics, response, and a strong community of writers (Newkirk & Kittle, 2013). Reading and writing, both digitally and in the traditional manner, are fundamental to my literacy block. They are the nonnegotiables.

Students have at least 30 minutes to read and write every day. When reading, they may be reading blogs and online articles on websites like Wonderopolis or DOGOnews (dogonews.com). Others will be reading traditional texts, both fiction and nonfiction. During writing workshop they may be gathering ideas in their writer's notebooks, drafting a story on paper, collaborating on a story via Google Docs, writing a blog, taking notes for their research, or revising a piece for publication. This second chunk of time is important for students to be able to get into the flow needed for deeper reading and writing.

Students are empowered when given choice in reading and writing, making the experience more authentic. Part of being a reader and writer is finding your passion and spending time exploring your ideas and interests. Throughout different genre studies, we have a range of topics in our classroom. We have narratives about spending time with grandparents, nail-biting sporting events, cooking disasters, and playing with beloved pets. Studies of informational writing bring a plethora of different topics: amazing predators, John Deere tractors, extreme weather, and the invention of bubble gum.

Unless writing in their own diaries, most writers want to write for an authentic, outside audience. Each day my students have the opportunity to respond to the other young writers in my classroom. It looks different on different days. Students may spend time in the author's chair and receive verbal feedback from other students. At other times, they may get comments on their latest blog entry from me or from someone in our virtual community. I am able to give students feedback when I confer with them either face-to-face or by adding comments to writing they've done in Google Docs. This response helps students move forward as writers as they refine their skills.

A strong community of writers (and readers, and scientists, and mathematicians) is essential to our classroom. Like many other teachers and writers, I believe that all writing is social. Children have ideas and they want to be heard. They need to know that their voices matter. It's also imperative that students feel safe to take risks. Sharing one's thinking and writing is risky. Adding the digital component expands our community to include even more people. Being able to collaborate and connect with others outside of our classroom walls has become a powerful element of our reading and writing workshops. Students know that they may be sharing their thinking and writing with students in another state or even another country.

DIGITAL MENTOR TEXTS

Before I ask my students to do any kind of writing in a new genre, we spend lots of time immersed in mentor texts (K. W. Ray, 2006). We begin the school year looking at different websites and blogs and charting what we notice. It's important for students to be able to navigate these texts as both readers and writers. Ralph Fletcher (2011) suggests that we approach mentor texts as "open source" pieces. "Instead of directing students to pay attention to this strategy or that technique, . . . *we invite them to look at these texts and enter into them on their own terms*" (p. 5, emphasis in original). I want my students to look at both the content and form (mode and media) when studying a piece of writing, be it digital or print. As is always the case, my students often notice things that I had not considered. For example, when we studied the KidsHealth website (kidshealth.org) closely, my students noticed:

- Layout
- Use of images

- Use of font and color
- Small chunks of text and white space
- Hyperlinks
- Use of video

Some things I hadn't considered that they thought important were:

- Use of humor (and what I call "the gross factor")
- Topic choice was especially relevant to kids' interests
- Articles written as if the author is talking to the audience

WONDEROPOLIS AS A DIGITAL MENTOR TEXT

Early in the year, I introduce the Wonderopolis website (wonderopolis. org), where we learn information on a different topic every day (for an example, see Figure 2.1). It is the perfect digital text in which to immerse my students. Through close study, my students soon recognize the familiar structure used in the Wonder of the Day page:

Figure 2.1. A Typical Wonderopolis Article

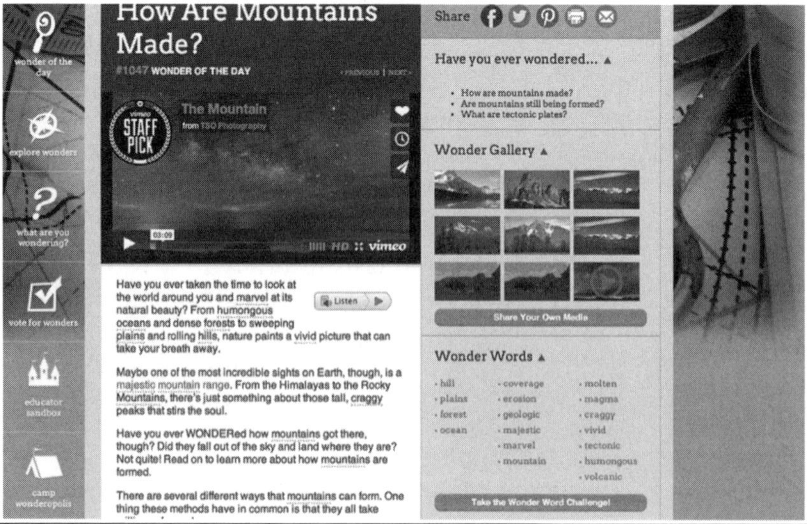

Wonderopolis image reproduced by permission.

- Begins with a question of the day
- Is followed by a video clip
- Is a short informational article with hyperlinks
- Has plenty of white space so that students can read chunks of information at a time
- Is written in a friendly, conversational tone that is inviting to its readers
- Includes a variety of images used to support the text and draw readers in
- Is set up so students learn domain-specific vocabulary through the supportive text
- Contains related links that allow readers to explore the topic even more
- Has a comment section
- Has a staff that will reply back within 24 hours

Besides the information provided in the articles, Wonderopolis is an outstanding example of a website that is easy to navigate. It becomes a mentor text for us as we learn about what 21st-century writing can look like in my classroom.

Impact of Digital Writing

Why digital writing? Our world is changing. The ways we read and write are changing. Overall, our students today have access to many different opportunities for reading, writing, and connecting with others than we did growing up. As a result, my role changes, too.

> Equipping students to write in only one mode—traditionally, black ink on white paper in scripted genres—will not serve students in their higher education experiences or in the workplaces of the future. Equipping students to work across and within contemporary networked spaces, and to write in a range of genres and a diversity of modes for audiences local and widespread, will serve students in their higher education experiences and in the workplaces of the future. (NWP et al., 2010, p. 5)

It becomes imperative that I am teaching my students not only how to be responsible digital citizens, but also how to craft their writing for the digital world.

Critical Literacy

My students are expected to gather information from both digital and print sources. In order to support them as critical consumers, I modified the key questions from the core principles page of the National Association for Media Literacy Education (NAMLE.net, 2007) and created these guidelines for evaluation:

> Who is the author of the website?
> Is the message factual or is it filled with opinions? What sources did the author cite?
> Who is the intended audience?
> Is the website easy to read and navigate?
> Are there a lot of ads?
> Is the content appropriate for children?

We used the above criteria to evaluate Wonderopolis, a website that we already knew was reliable. We then went to All About Explorers (allaboutexplorers.com) and looked at it with a critical eye. This is a great "fake" website to use with kids to show them just how a website that looks to be very authentic is, in fact, full of misinformation. Giving students opportunities like these to practice those critical thinking skills was an important part of the process.

Visual Literacy

In his book *I See What You Mean*, Steve Moline (2011) asserts that

> Information literacy is more than communicating with words, because many information texts also include visual elements, such as diagrams, graphs, maps, and tables. To provide a complete literacy program, therefore, we need to include opportunities to draw information as well as to write it. (p. 9).

From the time our children are very young, they understand that the "pictures" provide important information that supports the text. Visual elements are an integral component to informational texts, both print and online. I knew it was going to be important for students to look closely at the author's purpose of using visuals and how those visuals supported the overall structure of the text. We spent time reading nonfiction books and looking at different websites and online articles to determine how to best use different visuals. We also Skyped with a digital designer who gave us some advice about setting up our own webpage. We learned about the importance of white space and keeping information in short chunks so as not to lose our audience's attention. The impact of this close study and continued conversations can be seen throughout my students' work.

THE "WONDER" PROJECT

The Wonder project was our final research project of the year. We had done several mini research projects in the past, as well as learned many different tools for using technology not only to do research, but also to share our knowledge. The students were given free range (within reason) in their choice of topic. Allowing students choice is both scary and liberating. In the past I was used to assigning the traditional research projects that followed the same format. I asked students to answer the same questions, which may or may not have been what they were interested in learning. Giving students ownership in the inquiry process is paramount to its success. Some students needed guidance in choosing topics due to the lack of information available to them. We were able to tweak their ideas in order to find topics that were still interesting to them and honored their choice. When students are allowed to choose, they are motivated and self-driven. It makes their work real and purposeful.

Because Wonderopolis had been such a fundamental part of our classroom learning during the year, the students wanted to create a website that showcased their learning. All steps of the project were completed at school over a 6-week time period. If students chose to research or work on their drafts at home, they could, but it was not a requirement. Because I know that students are going to need support when completing a project like this, I do not assign it as homework. Instead, I collaborate with the media specialist and invite parent volunteers in to help us through each of the steps. This process, like all good teaching, gets messy. At any one time, students will be in different stages of the project.

We began by creating a modified KWL chart as suggested in *Energizing Research Reading and Writing* (Lehman, 2012). Instead of Know, Want to Know, and Learned, the three columns were labeled: Know a Lot About, Know Some About, and Know Little About. The difference in this chart is that the same topic was covered in each column. The students moved across the chart so that the ideas melded together (see Figure 2.2).

We then spent time looking for resources, narrowing our topic, identifying our audience, and gathering information. The breadth of topics was amazing to me. I had kids interested in researching different animals, space, Earth's layers, the evolution of video games, how to create apps, and bubble gum, to name a few. Because the students were able to pick topics in which they were interested, they were truly engaged in the whole process. I could feel the excitement in the room as they shared newly gained information and great resources. The kids were invested in this project.

Students used a variety of sources—including print, digital, and oral—to gather their information. In addition, they had choices in how they took their notes: using webs, sketching, jotting information using bullet points, and creating tables. We had spent a lot of time earlier in the year thinking about the purpose of different note-taking tools, and I wanted my students to be able to determine what would work for them as they gathered information about their topics. Many students used boxes and bullets. For instance, one student took notes using a flow chart when she studied how bubble gum was made, while another made detailed sketches with labels during his wildfire

Figure 2.2. Modified KWL Chart

Name: _____

Topic: _____

Know a Lot About	Know Some About	Know Little About

5-Minute Freewrite

research. Giving students control over their note-taking empowered them as researchers and authors.

Once they had completed their research, they needed to decide what visuals they would include in their webpages. Because we had spent so much time studying the visual components of informational text, my students had an understanding of choosing certain features for different reasons. Again, students were given choice in what they thought would best support their information. They even came up with their own ideas:

- Draw illustrations, photograph them, and then import them into their pages.
- Import images from the Internet.
- Photograph pages from books.
- Use Google Drawings to create timelines, diagrams, and images.

The students saved images in their Google Drive, along with all of the other information they had gathered.

While they worked on gathering images, they also had to draft their information. Drafting, collecting images, and designing the webpage were not linear processes. Each was going on in a different order in each student's project. This freedom made the project more authentic and engaging for the young researchers. For example, when writing this chapter, I drafted different sections at a time, not necessarily in the order that they would appear in the book.

Since the students were used to drafting their blogs directly on the computer, I decided to let them draft their research reports using Google Docs. They each created a research folder to share with me where they kept all of their information. Using Google Docs changed our work. I could give students feedback quickly by using the comments feature. Because Google Drive lives in the cloud, it is so easy to access student writing that is housed there. I didn't have to lug home a huge stack of writing folders. Instead, I could open my computer and have their work at my fingertips. I was able to give more frequent and timely feedback. My students were able to access my comments at home and make changes right then and there if they wanted to. Many students told me they felt as if we were having a back-and-forth conversation instead of being "graded" on their work. Another advantage is that the comments feature allows the author of the text to reply to comments. My students could ask clarifying questions in response to my feedback or explain more of their thinking. I also felt as if I could reach more students. My conferring wasn't confined to writing workshop time; it extended to those times when my students weren't sitting in my classroom.

The final step was for students to design their webpages. We would be using a template in Google Sites prepared by our technology teacher, and the kids could then decide where they wanted to put different elements such as hyperlinks, images, font changes, text, and color.

LOOKING CLOSELY AT CARSON'S PROJECT

I first looked at Carson's project about the layers of the Earth's crust from a very traditional view, focusing on the artifact itself. He had created a website, modeled after Wonderopolis, in which he described the way that the Earth was formed and how the different layers of the crust interact. I used a rubric for the initial assessment that included the following categories:

- Accuracy of information
- Visual features as they support the text
- Layout (use of white space, color, and graphics to organize the information)
- Links (included as needed, easy to navigate)
- Copyright (all sources are cited)
- Spelling and grammar

Going through the protocol discussion with our teacher inquiry group, I gleaned so much more information from my colleagues. They noticed things that I hadn't even considered, which opened my eyes to many new possibilities.

WHAT DO YOU NOTICE?

As our teacher inquiry group went through each round in the protocol, I realized how much deeper we could go in understanding

Carson's work compared to what I was able to do on my own using a standard rubric.

Carson's Use of Informational Text Features Along with Clear, Concise Sentences

A look at the overall webpage shows that Carson has an understanding of informational text features. His page is organized with a title, headings, information under each heading, and content vocabulary. In addition, he used a combination of text, charts, photos, and images that are both hand- and digitally drawn. He chose to use a descriptive text structure in his writing because he wanted to help his reader better "see" each of the Earth's layers. His lack of citations and hyperlinks suggests that he still does not understand the importance of these features when composing and publishing research.

The group had several insights about Carson's writing. His voice comes out clearly when he writes, "Earth's layers get warmer the deeper you go down." His description of the crust ("It has all the wrinkle scars in it") shows his attention to the image he chose. His work also shows our attention in class to content vocabulary. He integrates words like *mass, feet,* and *weight* in his piece. He goes back and forth between technical writing and procedural writing throughout the piece. One of my colleagues noted Carson's clear and concise sentences. Because the text and images work hand-in-hand, not as many words are needed to get the point across. The quick informational passages, although not lengthy, are enough to enable the reader to learn something. These short sentences are typical of the writing Carson did throughout the year.

Carson's Strategic Use of Visual Media

Carson spent a lot of time thinking about, creating, and organizing his images during class time. He uses a combination of images he drew by hand, photographed from a published book, created in a drawing application, and imported from the Internet. One of my colleagues described it as "museum-like." Another colleague noted that the hand drawing at the beginning of the webpage (see Figure 2.3) becomes an organizer for the entire piece. The multiple colors in the hand-drawn images are visually appealing to the reader. Carson's drawing of the

Figure 2.3. Carson's Diagram of the Earth's Formation

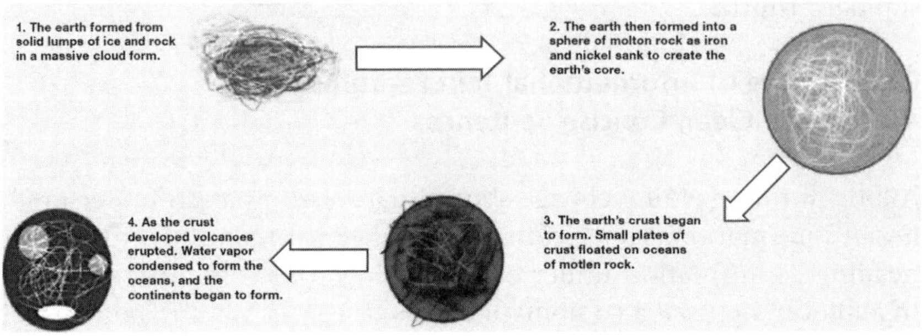

Google and the Google logo are registered trademarks of Google Inc., used with permission.

formation of the Earth's layers, done in Google Drawings, drew a lot of attention. His choice of using squiggly lines indicates movement and the chaotic process going on inside the earth. His use of color also indicates the different stages of the Earth's creation. He started with the warm colors red and yellow to symbolize the hot, molten rock. Blue begins to make its way into the drawing when the crust is formed, with the final image using blue and white to indicate the oceans and water vapor. The images that Carson chose also show that he was making sense of what he was reading and learning. He chose strong images to complement the text. Several of my colleagues noted that the interplay between the text and images created more meaning than either would on its own.

Carson's Understanding of Website Design

Carson's work showed the impact of the earlier work we had done when looking at mentors. In class we spent a lot of time studying mentor texts. We noticed moves that digital authors made and how those decisions impacted the reader. We specifically noticed, when we looked closely at mentor texts and talked with a web designer, that websites are set up so that the reader can read small chunks of information at a time. White space is used to create those chunks of text, as are visual images. Carson made conscious decisions in the layout of his information based on our earlier work. He is consistent in his headings—The Crust, The Mantle, The Core—and blue horizontal bars separate each section, making it easier for the reader to navigate the webpage (see Figure 2.4).

Figure 2.4. A Segment of Carson's Wonder Webpage

The Crust

The crust is made of Igneous, metamorphic, and sedimentary rocks. Under the ocean the crust may be 5 miles (8 km) thick. under the continents it can be 25 miles (40 km) deep or more. The crust is broken up into 15 pieces called plates. It has all of the wrinkles and scars in it.

The Mantle

The Mantle is made of silicon, magnesium, iron, aluminum,and oxygen. The upper and lower mantle combined are almost 1,800miles (2,253 km) thick. The lower mantle is heavier than the upper mantle because it has some iron in it. The mantle makes up 70% of the Earth's mass (weight).

Google and the Google logo are registered trademarks of Google Inc., used with permission.

QUESTIONS INVITE DEEPER THINKING

It soon became evident to me as we went through this process, especially during the questioning round, that my thinking about Carson's work needed to expand into examining more than the artifact itself. Those working with the National Writing Project's Multimodal Assessment Project recognized that there was much more to consider when assessing a student's digital work. They suggest assessing one of five different domains, which include the artifact, context, substance, process management, and habits of mind (MAP Group, 2013). Having looked at Carson's "Wonder Project" as an artifact above, I now turn my attention to the other four domains.

First, in terms of context, how did Carson take on the role of researcher and webpage designer? From the beginning, Carson took this assignment very seriously. He threw himself into the project quite enthusiastically. Any time he had the opportunity for independent reading, Carson chose to read nonfiction books and articles, both in print and online, that pertained to different science topics. He had a special interest in earth science, which helped him come to his topic. He read every single book in our "Earth" basket in the classroom library and always had a stack of similar titles from our school library on his desk. In fact, as we began to choose topics, Carson chose "Earth" as his area of study. When I encouraged him to dig a little deeper and ask himself what he would like to know more about, he quickly narrowed his topic to the Earth's layers. He diligently took notes and created visuals in a nonlinear fashion, keeping everything together in his research folder. Carson's interaction with Wonderopolis, the digital designer, nonfiction text features, visual literacies, and his content resources culminated in a final webpage that is informational as well as easy to navigate as he learned from his digital mentor texts.

Second, in terms of substance, how well does Carson get his message across to his audience? Carson's work shows that he made thoughtful decisions as he created his webpage. His information is accurate and he spent a considerable amount of time finding or creating images that would best support his text. In fact, he was so adamant that he needed the image of the Earth's core from *Time for Kids: Volcanoes* (Caplan, 2006) that he hounded me daily until I finally gave him my phone to take the photograph so that he could download and import it into his webpage. There are also areas where Carson's work could show improvement. He used a variety of sources, both print and digital, but he did not cite any of them. In addition, he did not make use of hyperlinks to direct his reader to other sites that would add depth to his information. The lack of these features lets me know that Carson (and others in my class) need more instruction on the importance and purpose of citing sources and using hyperlinks.

Third, in thinking about process management and technical skills, how did Carson take the technical skills he'd learned throughout the school year and apply them to this project? Before building his webpage, Carson created a mock-up of his webpage on paper. It was here that he decided how his webpage would appear, from the white space to the images to the font. These features show evidence that he had been composing digitally throughout the school year (blogging, collaborative word processing, digital storytelling). There is also room for growth. Carson chose to not add any hyperlinks, although he had used them in the past while blogging. In addition, he has some issues with spacing and separation of words.

Fourth, in terms of habits of mind, how does Carson show that he was an active learner in the creation of his webpage? Carson was engaged in this project from the beginning. He made purposeful decisions about each step of the process from choosing his topic, to how he took notes, to the images he used. He had a clear picture in his mind as to what he thought was important to share with his audience and how he could best demonstrate his learning. Carson was also not afraid to try new things with technology. When I showed him and a few other students the basics of Google Drawings, he jumped in and started exploring what he might create without any hesitation. His small group worked together to discover all of the possibilities with Drawings and then became the experts in our room.

REFLECTION ON THE PROCESS

Digital reading and writing was a huge motivator for Carson. Choice was also important to him. Carson is an intense child who loves science and learning new things. Having access to tools to help him share his learning gave him and others like him opportunities to create, publish, and share writing that he wouldn't otherwise have been able to do. The digital world opened up so many more possibilities for him. As an author, he knew what he needed to showcase his learning and was engaged throughout the whole process.

I learned so much going through this process. First and foremost, I learned the power in working collaboratively to assess student writing. Looking closely at Carson's work caused a paradigm shift in my thinking, as it helped me reflect not only on the assignment, but also on how I think about my students' work. This protocol became much bigger than a one-time assessment. It became part of my formative assessment that is woven throughout my instruction. As stated in NCTE's Position Statement, *"Formative Instruction That* Truly *Informs Instruction,"*

> Formative assessment is a constantly occurring process, a verb, a series of events in action, not a single tool or a static noun. In order for formative

assessment to have an impact on instruction and student learning, teachers must be involved every step of the way and have the flexibility to make decisions throughout the assessment process. (NCTE Assessment Task Force, 2013, p.3)

I find that I am more keenly aware of the digital moves individual students are making. In addition, these close observations allow me to have deeper discussions and ask strategic questions as I build my assessment into our writing conferences and any other conversations we might have throughout the day.

In reflecting on the assignment, it was evident that I needed to provide more minilessons on the importance of citing sources and how to cite correctly. I also needed to allow more time for the design process and build in more check-ins to ensure that students were including all of the required components. In the original project, our technology teacher designed the site, making decisions for the students. The second time, I used Weebly (weebly.com) and gave students complete control of layout decisions. Many of our writing conferences centered around those decisions. We had multiple conversations about why they made the digital moves they did, which is an important part of the process. Weebly also allowed members outside of our classroom to leave comments. Connecting with others is a huge motivating factor in digital work. It's the world we live in today.

I also kept going back to the question, "What would happen if we let kids go through this collaborative assessment process?" I reflected back on the question asked by NWP's Multimodal Assessment Project team: "What would the assessment of digital writing look like if we began conversations between writers and readers, students and teachers, children and adults?" (MAP, 2013). I believe that 4th-graders could be taught to go through this process. It leaves me with more questions, though: How much time would it take to teach this process well? Would students be able to give valuable feedback? How would going through this process help kids become better digital composers?

In addition, now that I've gone through the protocol with other teachers, I want to continue. There was a lot of power in going through the protocol with others in the group. Having not gone through this process before, I was a little nervous at first. I quickly learned that this experience was going to be nothing but positive. The purpose of using this protocol was to ask a group of professionals to look at a piece of work objectively and to give their insight. My colleagues were respectful of my student's work as they looked at it in a positive, non-threatening manner. I left our first protocol meeting feeling energized by the whole process.

At this point, I am left wondering. The power of collaboration, looking closely at student compositions, and having time for reflection was phenomenal. At the same time, the time commitment for one piece of writing is substantially more than what is required using a traditional rubric. How do we manage to assess every student? Do we aim for each student to receive this type of feedback once or twice a year and try to do a few students each grading period? How do we show teachers the potential in thinking about student work in this way? These are questions I'm willing to explore because I so strongly believe in this protocol.

CHAPTER 3

Nurturing Middle School Readers Through Reviews and Book Trailers

Jeremy Hyler

Chippewa River Writing Project (Michigan)

digitalis.nwp.org/resource/6270

I have been a teacher for almost 15 years at a small rural school in the middle of the state of Michigan. Our entire 7–12 building consists of around 500 students. In our small middle school I am the entire language arts department. For the last 4 years I have been teaching both 7th- and 8th-grade students. I see three sections of 7th-grade students and two sections of 8th-grade students each day. On average, I see about 110 students on a daily basis. Our middle school is on a traditional schedule that has four 9-week marking periods. Students start each day with an advisory class for 18 minutes and then have six classes that each last about an hour. Students have math, language arts, social studies, science, and two elective classes. Students then go to physical education, band, or health the last hour of their day.

In addition to my teaching duties, I have been a National Writing Project Consultant since 2010 through the Chippewa River Writing Project at Central Michigan University. During this time I have had the privilege of working with dynamic individuals concerning the shift in classrooms when it comes to digital literacies. Troy Hicks, a profound leader and author in digital literacies, has been a mentor to me as a writer and teacher. In addition, he coauthored a book with me titled *Create, Compose, Connect! Reading, Writing and Learning with Digital Tools* (Hyler & Hicks, 2014), where we examined the use of digital tools in my own classroom. During the summer of 2013 I attended a weeklong Summer Institute in Digital Literacies hosted by Renee Hobbs and Rhode Island's Harrington School of Communication and Media. While there as a participant and a presenter, we looked at the changes in literacy, the purpose and application of the various digital tools available for teachers to use, and ways to apply our knowledge and skills using those same digital tools and technologies.

Using the knowledge I have gained from the work done with the National Writing Project, Troy, and the digital literacy institute, I provide them a place to learn, experiment, be creative, and discover how they can extend what they have learned using various digital tools and technologies along with multimodel assessment (MAP Group, 2013) and the Framework for Success in Postsecondary Writing (CWPA et al., 2011).

Whether students are reading an actual book or reading on their phone, tablet, or any other device, I am a firm believer that even the most reluctant middle school readers can be nurtured and develop appreciation for literature and reading. Kelly Gallagher (2009) states in his book *Readacide* that we have been killing our students' interest in reading by constantly bombarding them with worksheets and boring classroom lectures.

Recent publications from advocates of adolescent reading such as Penny Kittle (2013), Kylene Beers and Robert Probst (2012), and Jeff Wilhelm and Bruce Novak (2011) demonstrate the salience of this perennial topic and remind me that I am not alone in my struggles to motivate struggling readers. On the other hand, teaching 7th- and 8th-grade students has challenges all on its own: Adding reading and the implementation of the Common Core State Standards into the classroom while trying to help students interpret and effectively understand digital literacies could make a teacher's head spin. However, if we don't meet our students at the door, willing to show them how literacy has transformed in the digital age, we will continue to see more and more students become disengaged with our lessons, units, and projects.

In terms of writing curriculum, a genre that often gets little attention as students progress through middle school and into high school is narrative. Often, the focus in the classroom shifts to informational and argumentative types of reading and writing. Thankfully, one of the CCSS writing genres focuses around narrative reading and writing. Since introducing the Common Core standards into my classroom, I have planned out my year in such a way that the students explore one of the three genres for each marking period, and in the last marking period we work on a multigenre project where students create argumentative, narrative, and informational pieces.

At the beginning of the year, we start digging deeper into the narrative genre. My 8th-graders begin reading *The Outsiders* by S. E. Hinton (1967). Throughout the whole unit, no matter what lesson or activity that I am doing with my students, they love the book and are genuinely excited about reading, often begging me to let them read more on their own so they can find out what happened in the story. I have been starting with this book every year since I started teaching 8th grade. In addition, over the past 4 years, I have been integrating various technologies into my existing lesson plans to help foster creativity in my students. We use Schoology (schoology.com/home.php), a social media tool similar to Facebook (facebook.com), or Edmodo (edmodo.com) to have discussions about *The Outsiders*. From time to time I might lead a discussion in which students need to respond to my prompt or question. Students also direct their own conversation using a set of standards adapted from our high school English 10 class (Figure 3.1).

I enjoy using social media tools like Schoology because everyone gets involved, students are more engaged because it mirrors Facebook, and we have more in-depth conversations. Since my students always seem to flourish with *The Outsiders*, I want to capture their excitement and have my students carry this enthusiasm forward by encouraging them to read more narrative texts outside of the classroom.

While trying to encourage my students to do more reading on their own, I try to give them access to many choices for reading that can spark their interest into picking up a book for pleasure. Without those choices, students are less likely to open the front cover of a book. I have incorporated ideas such as reading aloud from a novel to my students daily, visiting the library, allowing students to use tablets and other devices for reading, digital literature circles, producing alternate endings with comic strip apps such as Toondoo (toondoo.com), and creating book trailers using a tool called Animoto (animoto.com), which has not been a part of the curriculum in the past. In short, my goal of creating enthusiasm for reading seems to be going well.

Figure 3.1. Expectations for Online Book Discussions

1. Post at least one thoughtful discussion question to your group. DO NOT REPEAT A QUESTION THAT HAS ALREADY BEEN POSTED.
2. Here on Schoology, respond thoughtfully in writing to at least TWO of your classmates' question/comments. When responding to your classmates, reply below their comment or question. DON'T START A NEW DISCUSSION THREAD! It will make it easier to follow the discussion. Use the person's name when responding to someone specific. For example, "Jimmy, I never thought of it that way. I was thinking . . ."
3. Do your best to demonstrate thoughtful interaction with the text and your classmates. Compliment strong points, ask questions, and build on ideas shared. Below are some ways you can add to the discussion:
   a. Present a new question to refine or redirect discussion
   b. Share a personal experience that relates to the book
   c. Think outside the box/play devil's advocate
   d. Ask for clarification
   e. Share another resource
   f. Summarize main ideas presented
   g. Comment thoughtfully
4. "Check in" on the discussion at least twice (NOT including your original question posting), with at least 12 hours between your first and last post.
5. Do your best to write as clearly and correctly as possible. (NO TEXT TALK). DON'T PROCRASTINATE! :)

Still, something seems to be missing. I want my students to think critically and deeply about a particular book without having them do a traditional book report or having them keep track of any reading in a reading log. In the past these types of requirements had tended to stifle (actually, stomp out) student interest. There is no way I want to dampen the enthusiasm they are showing, yet they need to be held accountable for reading thoughtfully and making connections with the text. And, as we continue to debate and define the idea of "close reading" from the CCSS, students have to demonstrate a clear understanding of characters, plot, conflict, and other narrative elements such as the different literary devices an author uses.

One way to accomplish this deeper reading came from an idea discussed with a former colleague. I modified it for the level I was teaching. It called for students to do a book review rather than a book report. Although it is still more traditional in the sense of writing, I was drawn to it because I could require my students to use media (e.g., a picture of the book cover) and I could require them to add links within their review. Although there is no single correct way to write a book review, I wanted my students to keep in mind that a book review is not a book report, and I wanted them to understand the purpose of incorporating visual literacies, as well as placing links in their writing. I wanted their audience, who would be me and their fellow classmates, to know if the book is something they would enjoy and why they would enjoy it.

The book review was an interesting alternative to a traditional book report and it got my students writing more, yet it still seemed as though it wasn't enough to help students fully realize their potential as readers and writers. In addition, I wasn't able to see any of their creativity shine through in a Google document. They needed to take ownership of their learning. Moreover, as I became more engaged in my understanding of digital writing, I began to wonder how students might use visual media more effectively to convey their ideas. As Steve Moline (2011) believes, "There are times when it makes sense not to write information in sentences. Visual texts sometimes do the job better" (p. 10). I wanted to think about when, how, and why students could combine digital media elements into their interpretations of the book. Furthermore, I wanted students to have multimodal assessments of their writing.

So last year I took their book project a step further and gave my students two choices when it came to doing a multimodal response. Students could choose between making a comic strip using Toondoo or creating a digital book trailer using Animoto. Toondoo is an online site where students can create comic strips, and Animoto is a cloud-based site where individuals can create videos using pictures, music, video, and backgrounds. Ninety percent of my students chose to do the book trailer artifact using Animoto.

THE PROJECT: USING ANIMOTO FOR A MULTIMODAL RESPONSE

When I introduced Animoto at the beginning of the project, I showed students different digital book trailers or artifacts that other middle school students had created themselves using the digital tool. Some of the videos that were shown were from students I had taught in the past. After we watched two or three videos, I asked the students to take out their journals. We then watched the videos a second time through, and I asked the students to write down what they noticed in each one of the videos that had been created. We were looking specifically for elements of author's craft represented in this piece of digital writing (Hicks, 2013), for example, what creative elements the author used when creating the video. Students pointed out elements in the video such as music, background, words being used, and pictures. (Figure 3.2 shows the content of a Google document that one of the classes used for collaboration and brainstorming.)

From there we discussed what elements they needed to have in their own videos. Table 3.1 outlines the guidelines my students have for their digital book trailers, compared with the guidelines that I had previously offered for a written book review.

After discussing the guidelines students must follow, I gave students a 50-minute class period to sign up for Animoto and to play with the digital tool so they could see how it works; that gives them sufficient time to ask any questions that may arise. I have found in the last 2 years that this is more than enough time for students to play around with the features of Animoto, and simple tasks like choosing a background, writing text, and inserting pictures can be modeled for students in less than 15 minutes. One must keep in mind, though, that with the free version students are limited with respect to some of the features of the tool. Students are limited to certain music and backgrounds. In addition, students are only allowed to make 30-second videos. If a teacher wants students to create longer videos and have access to more content, Animoto offers plus and pro pricing plans.

Now, fast-forward to a few weeks before spring break, and my introduction of the book project. I hand out the guidelines to my students and walk them through models from prior years. Students must choose a chapter book that not only is appropriate for their reading

Figure 3.2. Class Brainstorm of Elements of Digital Craft in Animoto Videos

Video is 32 seconds
It has music
There are pictures
The video has words in it
There are different colors
There is a title
The author's name is at the beginning
Music is upbeat
Writing is short and to the point

Table 3.1. Criteria for Book Review and Book Trailer

Written Book Review (Fiction)	Digital Book Trailer Using Animoto (Fiction)
You are a book reviewer. Your audience is potential readers who are possibly interested in the book.	You are now the producer of a video book trailer for the book you read. Think about your potential readers. You have 30 seconds!
• Top center of your paper: The book's title and author, publisher, year published, number of pages, written at the top of the review	Sign up for an account at animoto. com (see me if you were absent). Take time to play around with Animoto's features first. Get familiar with the tool. Your book trailer should be 30 seconds in length. Think about the type of music that can relate to your book.
• 1st Paragraph: A brief summary of the plot that does not give away too much. Leave the reader in suspense about major conflict resolutions while painting a clear, interesting portrait of the novel's story.	
• 2nd Paragraph: Character analysis. Are the main characters believable? Do you know anyone like them? Does the author adequately describe the characters? Does the author do a good job of revealing characters' thoughts and feelings?	• Text: Include your title at the beginning or end of your video, and short blurbs about the book.
	• Pictures of the book cover and other pictures related to the book should be included in your trailer.
• 3rd Paragraph: Comparison/contrast to another novel, poem, or movie (character, themes, setting, historical relevance, conflict, societal issues/topics, emotion, tone, writing style, or author's personal values).	• Your book trailer should have no mistakes! Use correct, spelling, grammar, and punctuation.
• 4th paragraph: Comments on the book's strengths and weaknesses (List at least one of each).	• Book trailers should be a snapshot or sneak peak into what the book is about. Do not give away key plot points to potential readers (think about a movie trailer).
• 5th paragraph: The reviewer's personal response to the book, with specific examples from the book provided as support.	• Check out YouTube for more examples. Search book trailers!
	• It must be school-appropriate!

level, but also has over 100 pages. And, because I am a big advocate for giving chances for students to be creative, Animoto and the digital book trailer not only can allow students to express themselves, but also offer—within the landscape of differentiated instruction—a different way to assess students in relation to the multimodal assessment:

Context: How the artifact the student creates fits into the world

Process management and technique: How the artifact was planned, created, and circulated or distributed

Habits of mind: What types of behaviors and attitudes can be nurtured throughout the process

Even with a detailed explanation, students will have questions throughout the project. Here are the topics I discuss and review with my students during the introduction to the project:

- How can you describe the setting, sequence of events in the story, climax, and the resolution?
- How do authors create characters? Students continue their thinking on how characters have physical and emotional features and characteristics—flat versus round characters. How would the story be different if it were told from a different character's perspective?
- What is the theme or the central idea(s) being taught by the author? With the adaptation of the CCSS, students need to: "determine two or more central ideas in a text and analyze their development over the course of the text; provide an objective summary of the text" (RL.7.2, corestandards.org/ ELA-Literacy/RL/7/2/). Even after I discuss this topic many times, middle school students often struggle with finding multiple themes and noting how theme is developed over the course of the text. As more complex texts are read and discussed, students cannot make the appropriate connections to real life or understand what the author may be teaching them.
- What literary elements does the author use to enhance the reader's experience, such as symbolism and figurative language like similes, metaphors, or personification? Why is the author's craft important?
- Does this book remind you of other books, ideas, movies, or events in your life? What connections can you make to real life?

The elements we discuss should essentially be a review for the students. Each particular area was highlighted in earlier units of reading prior to the project. This list of review elements and questions then leads into the requirements for the written book review and the book trailer (see Table 3.1). They work on both the written review and the digital book trailer at the same time.

In comparison to the written report, the book trailer may appear to be less demanding for students. However, when students are creating a digital piece, they must consider things such as background, pictures, text, and music. Since the digital book trailer is a completely different genre of writing, I tell students that the requirements can potentially change slightly, depending on how students choose to express themselves. Animoto is a user-friendly, yet complex, digital tool; it can help deepen a student's understanding of a given assignment. For example, every student producing a book trailer could potentially make better connections with the genre. They can accomplish this by not only generally describing the genre in the written book review, but they could discover other books or genres that the given author might have written by putting a link in the report. This would allow potential readers to get a feel for the book by the music and pictures that have been used. Again, this could potentially help others gain more interest in reading. In addition, my hope was that my students would engage deeply in visual literacies. Visual literacies are gaining significant momentum in the literature world, and Animoto could be another portal into increased excitement with reading, especially with middle school students.

Thus my students embarked on their spring break with their book in hand and the goal in mind of creating a digital representation of their reading and completing a book review as a way to share their thinking.

INSIGHTS FROM THE COLLABORATIVE
ASSESSMENT CONFERENCE PROTOCOL

For the Collaborative Assessment Conference protocol completed online with the other authors of this book, I shared Lauren's digital book trailer and written book review. Lauren was an 8th-grader at the time. She chose to read the book *Crossed* by Ally Condie (2011), the second book in the *Matched* series, a dystopian trilogy in the same spirit as *The Hunger Games*. I invite the reader to look at Lauren's Animoto video on the Digital Is website and ask yourself the following questions before reading my reflections on the protocol discussion.

- What do you see or notice?
- What questions does this work raise for you?
- What works well for you in each piece of Lauren's work?

The protocol and insights gained from my colleagues helped me understand that Lauren did a solid job of completing both of her assignments. However, the assignment could have been richer by teaching students about visual literacies. Furthermore, teaching my students what it means to extend their ideas is important. I will approach each of these insights in turn.

Noticing What My Student Did with Her Digital Writing

As my colleagues discussed my student's' work in the collaborative assessment conference protocol, they identified a number of effective components that were evident in both pieces the student completed (see Table 3.2).

Explicit Teaching of Visual Literacies

As you can see, during the time my colleagues looked at Lauren's work, they found multiple positives of the work my student completed. However, taking a more direct approach with visual literacies was the most important idea I took away from the collaborative assessment. Today's learners are bombarded with images through Facebook, Twitter, text messages, and other forms of media. Teaching visual literacies will continue to be important in today's classroom so they can interpret, understand, and evaluate images. Visual literacies should guide students' thinking and provide them with ideas of why authors, illustrators, and photographers choose certain photos to use. In addition, they should consciously think about what story is trying to be told with the pictures. As an educator, teaching my students how to interpret those pictures can provide them with a skill they can take beyond school and into their world as consumers and employers.

Lauren, the 8th-grader who completed these two pieces, did accomplish a few important elements, although our guess is that she did so quite subconsciously and with the help of a template from Animoto. She did a great job balancing the images with the text throughout the video. And the text itself provided a nice contrast to the various

Table 3.2. Qualities Identified in Lauren's Book Review and Book Trailer

Written Book Review	Digital Book Trailer
• Gives me enough detail to want to read the book • For an 8th-grade book review, this is very good—the writing here, while not perfect, is very engaging. When I first saw it, I thought "oh no" but I was taken by it, especially at the end with the comparison to *Hunger Games* and the evaluation—this takes it beyond plot summary • Rich descriptions that really work to bring the book to light and to enlighten us as to what the book feels like to read—hair, scars • Getting into the critique aspect of the essay—getting into her thinking and to actually address it • The student's handling of a complex plot that was narrated for someone who had not read the book. • Strong sense of audience, enthusiasm moving through both—but with different strategies for audio, video, and other forms. What does persuasive writing look like in two different modes? • Her treatment of the genre of dystopian lit is interesting—her ability to make connections is interesting with all the concepts from the book about society, dealing with insanity with panache	• The music complemented the video very well • The text was up long enough to be read, but at the same time the combination of slides and text moved quickly to capture the tension of the story • The combination of the review and the trailer worked well—it is a big challenge to take a long piece of text and to boil it down to just a few lines. Doing this simultaneously is great • The text and video work well together—it showed me what the author could do, and it also gave us another entry point into the book. The text and the video serve as two entry points, along with the hyperlink to the author's website • Convinces the viewer to want to get the book—persuasive undertone • Trailer with review—journalism changing a bit and how the expectations are changing • "Predators"—writers, editors, and producers—packaging it all together • Choice of images was powerful • The student's rhetorical strategy of picking up on an idea that is hot—timeliness. Ethos, fascinating how rhetorically savvy she is.

backgrounds as the video progressed (see Figure 3.3a). The other pictures, such as the bright lights and the geometric shapes throughout the video, helped set the tone for the book (see Figure 3.3b). Finally, the visual of the front cover of the book was appropriate for trying to entice potential readers (see Figure 3.3c).

Figure 3.3. Images in Lauren's Video Book Trailer

A: Introduction to Lauren's Animoto Video

At 0:04 seconds into the video, Lauren introduces part of the setting.

B: Introducing the Main Conflict of the Novel

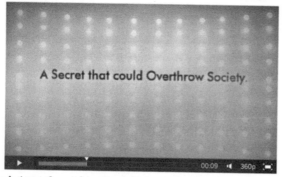

At 0:09 seconds into the video, Lauren introduces the conflict.

C: Concluding the Video with the Title and Book Cover

As the video nears its end, Lauren displays the title and book cover (cover image blurred to avoid rights violation).

When it came to the written book review where the students added links, I had envisioned them connecting to an author's webpage,
a link to a written essay they have composed, and perhaps even a
link to a book review that could be an audio recording on YouTube.
In addition, I wanted students to add images to their book review, for
instance, an image of the front cover of the book. The conclusion of
Lauren's book review is shown in Figure 3.4. By asking my students to
produce a fuller, more complex text to complement their digital book
trailer, I feel that I could get them closer to the metacognition that I
was hoping for with this project, an idea I will expand on a bit more
below. Also, with adding links and images to their document, they are
creating a more authentic piece of writing that can be shared with a
broader audience, not just their teacher.

Figure 3.4. The Conclusion of Lauren's Book Review

Evaluation:

This book, for me, receives four out of five stars. Condie really does so well
at describing the characters and the setting of the book, it feels as if she has
immersed us into the book and into the world within and outside of Society.
Condie uses such great detail to describe a river area in the plains during
a bombing: "The force of the explosion has thrown earth into the stream
and dammed it. Turned it into pools. Little pieces of river with nowhere to
run." She also can clearly describe what goes on within the minds of the
main characters, like when Ky finds a friend dead after an explosion: "I
look at those empty eyes that reflect back the blue of the sky because there
is nothing left of (spoiler) himself." Condie also intermingled paintings
and poems from before even our generation was born. This gives the book
a sort of old-fashioned reminiscence that the readers will love. She uses
Cassia to describe the painting *Chasm of the Colorado*, and Condie also uses
excerpts from Tennyson's poem *Crossing the Bar* and Dylan Thomas's *Do Not
Go Gentle into that Good Night*. The only thing that I wish that Condie could
have done better with would be to get certain events done and over with
so that we could get to the next major event. For example, Cassia and Ky
found a cavern in which Society kept skin samples of Citizens on the day
of their Final Banquet, and that pretty much took up one chapter. I felt
that she could have made events like those a lot bigger. But other than that
fatal flaw, Condie has impressed me once again with her romance story of
Cassia and Ky as they battle Society to stay together. This story is the perfect
romance, but it also doses in some sci-fi action.

Extending Ideas

When considering the idea of students attaching a more formal writing piece to their digital book trailers, I ask them to do so using Google Drive. As with all thoughtful writing projects, this essay deepens their thinking. Students could potentially write a persuasive essay convincing others to read their book, reviewing and helping solidify the unit on public service announcements. Alternatively, students could compose an informational piece that compares and contrasts the book they read to another book written by the same author, a writing assignment that can also help reinforce what was learned earlier in the year. Both of these ideas, however, could tend to force students back into the "book report" mode of thinking, where simple summaries are shared in lieu of deeper thinking about the text. This assignment could potentially lead to the flexibility of students choosing an appropriate assessment that connects to the curriculum.

In particular, as I revise this project for the future, I want to look at the original assignment criteria. In short, I realized that I was only having students share the most basic elements of the story with their audience, not asking them to think critically about how the visual elements that they included could affect the overall significance of their project. As I think about how to encourage them to make these deeper connections, I want them to keep asking the question "Why?" Why is this author using a certain literary device? Why is the author choosing this particular picture instead of a different one? Why does the author vary sentence, paragraph, and chapter length?

As my students think about these questions and dig deeper into literacy, I want them to apply the same skills they are learning with a project such as this one to other projects done digitally. With technology becoming an integral part of every classroom, students should understand the importance of using appropriate and meaningful pictures, backgrounds, and music in video. Our students are becoming composers of many modes of writing with more and more access to digital content, and they should know how to create those pieces effectively to reach their audiences.

IMPLICATIONS FOR FUTURE INSTRUCTION AND ASSESSMENT

Though I feel the assignment went well, I can see now where I can make some significant improvements.

First, in terms of using Animoto, there were both academic issues related to the substance of student work and also technical difficulties. In my school district, just over 70% of my students have access to the Internet on a device other than a cell phone. Due to this statistic, more students struggle getting the assignment done outside of school. Fortunately, my students have access to a mobile lab cart and can complete most of the assignment in school. However, lack of technology access does not usually take away from being able to move forward with the project. This has not only made me think critically about *when* to do the project, but it has also made me think about how I can effectively use class time to meet individual student needs. If I invite students to do the reading over spring break, then come back with notes and ideas for their digital book trailer, we can spend a few days talking about effective visual design while, at the same time, they are writing deeper analyses of their books.

Second, in terms of the assignment criteria, I recognize the need to define both process and product. Originally, I created a rubric that was mostly based on specific attributes of the written book review and the digital book trailer, but not necessarily on the quality of those attributes. Thus, in terms of having a rubric, I decided on creating a structure for students where they can work within guidelines, not a rubric. I feel a rubric doesn't give the freedom for students to be creative and it doesn't allow them to explore different possibilities for meeting the criteria set before them. A rubric forces students to meet certain expectations, and there is no room for them to go "outside the box." If students don't reach what is required of them in a rubric, they lose points. Guidelines don't necessarily do this. Furthermore, I don't feel a rubric can capture the process and product that must be reflected. While the rubric and the guidelines will have a number of the same criteria, I might also consider ways to help students answer the "why" questions throughout their work, and make a specific purpose for the digital book trailer as a whole, as well as the components in the video. This could include the purposeful links to outside material such as author pages and other books with the same genre that are put into the student's book review. This process would also include an additional reflection, one in which students justified their choices.

MOVING FORWARD/REFLECTION

While I was a bit nervous at the beginning of the CAC process, having multiple perspectives on the students' work helped me see that there are many other possibilities with this project. By having high school, middle school, and college educators look at my work and my lesson in general, I gained insight into what other teachers would want out of their students, and I gained valuable information on how to better prepare my middle school students for high school and even college. In short, the process was phenomenal for me as a teacher, knowing now how I can help my students improve their work by creating better assignments. In making myself vulnerable, opening up one of my students' assignments—an assignment that I had previously thought was very good—to critique, I realized that I was not assessing my students on everything that was important, especially in the world of digital literacy.

Reflecting back on the digital pieces that Lauren composed and the CAC process in relation to digital literacies, my students now complete their written book reviews on a class blog I created using Edublogs (edublogs.org). After listening to the feedback that I received, I felt the students needed to write for a more authentic audience. In addition, I try to take a day for the class to watch the digital book trailers all of the students have created. Students bring in popcorn and candy, and it is almost like we are watching a movie. The students really enjoy it, and there is a broader audience for their work. The assignment Lauren completed did not allow her to submit her work for an authentic audience. Therefore, she didn't reach as many potential readers, especially ones outside of our school.

Besides considering more authentic audiences, I want my students to experience the CAC process. This past year my students engaged in the process on a small assignment posted on Schoology. Students were broken into smaller groups and were given the CAC protocol after it was modeled for them as a whole class. The biggest takeaway from students engaged in the process was the rich conversations that took place among the students within their groups and when we reconvened as a whole class. It gave students a new way to think about what their classmates were doing. Furthermore, it pulled them out of the rut of doing the typical revision/editing process that normally occurs with their classmates' writing or work.

In addition, based on what my colleagues noticed, I feel that I could have done a better job of directing my students about choosing specific visuals for their digital book trailers and helping them choose what text to write in the limited time and characters they had. For instance, I had never considered talking with them about the difference between choosing a black and white photo compared to one that has color, or what they could write without revealing too much about the book but still hook potential readers. Furthermore, though multimodal assessments are being used, it doesn't guarantee that my students are going to jump up and start reading books on their own. However, students become more engaged because a book review and a book trailer are more authentic. Students start to develop more of a curiosity and develop more openness to ways of being assessed. All in all, I want to continue to improve my instruction in relation to the digital pieces being created within digital spaces by my students. Digital literacy continues to grow in importance for our students, and it is vital for teachers to emerge as leaders to help guide students in the right direction.

CHAPTER 4

"Seize the Day"

Finding Voice by Creating Public Service Announcements

Bonnie Kaplan
Jack Zangerle
Hudson Valley Writing Project (New York)

digitalis.nwp.org/resource/6290

Katie was one of those quiet kids who came to school every day and did what was expected of her. But she was a digital creator in the confines of her bedroom, making movies on her Macbook that she shared with friends. If Will Richardson, well-known tech educator, had run into Katie when he was researching his recent wake-up call for teachers in the United States entitled "Why School?" and asked her if she thought that school was offering her valuable learning opportunities in the digital world, she might have smirked, shrugged, and then responded, "No way!" The timing was perfect—we were entering the second year of the Inquiry Community (IC) project at Dover Middle School just as she was entering the 8th grade.

> In this new story, real learning happens anytime, anywhere, with anyone we like—not just with a teacher and some same-age peers, in a classroom, from September to June. More important, it happens around the things we learners choose to learn, not what someone else tells us to learn. (Richardson, 2012, Kindle Locations 62–64)

Jack Zangerle, 8th-grade English language arts teacher at Dover Middle School and education technology enthusiast, entered the 2011 school year attempting to create something unique for the 8th-grade class. Inspired by a program in character education he had observed in an inner-city school in the Bronx, New York, and with an administrative green light, he began to flesh out his plans with Matt Pool, the social studies teacher on the 8th-grade team, and Bonnie Kaplan, a codirector of the Hudson Valley Writing Project, who couldn't wait to take the plunge with them.

Over the course of the next 2 years, all 8th-graders would meet regularly in small inquiry communities with their 8th-grade teachers. Each inquiry group would take on a local problem in the Dover community in need of solving, study it, and raise awareness about the issue.

To support these inquiry groups, the teacher team met with Bonnie, who modeled literacy strategies. Additionally, Jack selected a student team composed of tech-savvy kids, representing each IC group, who would work with Bonnie and Jack on multimodal projects that they would share with their communities. For an overview, you can watch our video of "Year One"(vimeo.com/25464428).

We learned a lot in our first year of this IC project and, like the birth of a second child, in year 2 we were able to breathe more, demand more, and offer more student leaders opportunities for ownership.

During our first meeting with our newly formed technology team, the group of 12 student technology enthusiasts were surprised that Katie had not been included and urged us to invite her. We were thrilled to have the team take ownership so quickly. Even though Jack had Katie in one of his English classes, her passion for digital exploration came as a pleasant surprise to both of us. While student-owned mobile devices were not used in school, Katie's true learning began when she left the school, returned home to her own bedroom, and opened her window to the world of digital creation.

Our hope was, as Canadian education researcher Stephen Downes maintains, that "we have to stop thinking of an education as something that is delivered to us and instead see it as something we create for ourselves" (quoted in Richardson, 2012, Kindle Location 126 of 620).

Katie was thrilled by the invitation to join the tech team and arrived early for the next team session. She seemed comfortable but still reluctant to draw attention to herself. While the rest of the team opted to work with partners, Katie chose to work on her own. At each tech session the group left with homework assignments that pushed them to blend writing and digital tools in the creation of multimodal projects such as 5-image stories and digital stories that they would create and then share at the next team session.

Early in the year some of these assignments were very procedural. Using the 5-image story framework, students created pieces that visually depicted how to wash their hands or make cookies or pancakes. But as students evaluated their own work on these pieces and became more comfortable with the idea of communicating using images, we began to push them to create messages that conveyed deeper meanings. This is where members of the tech team began to tackle tough issues such as substance abuse and divorce. The stories they shared forced team members to look at how these images could be used to connect to the audience in an emotional way that further enriched the piece.

As the team began sharing their projects, everyone was wowed by Katie's experiments. It wasn't just her comfort with the digital tools, but how she used them to tell her stories. Now publishing to an authentic audience of her peers on the tech team, Katie basked in the praise and offered keen feedback to other members of the group in return. Recently reflecting on her experience, Katie said:

> I didn't talk much, but it really helped a lot. It gave me a specific path instead of a vague kind of thing in front of 23 kids it was more like 10 kids. The smaller group was more focused on me and the other kids.

In working with Katie, it became apparent that her work spoke much more loudly than she did. As we reflected on her work as teachers, it occurred to us that looking at her work in retrospect would help us understand her process as a learner and a creator and inform our teaching practice moving forward.

KATIE AS A DIGITAL LEARNER

Katie's experience is important to consider because she was living the life of a connected learner. According to the Connected Learning website (connectedlearning.tv), connected learning is "active, relevant, real-world, effective, hands on, networked, innovative, personal, and transformative" (connectedlearning.tv/infographic). The work that Katie was doing outside of the classroom represented so many of these principles. She had taught herself to use iMovie by diving in and trying it on her own. Like so many other young learners today, when she became stuck on a particular skill or technique, she reached out across the globe to a variety of mentors on tutorial sites. Katie knew that she wanted to create videos for her friends, and she put the time in to develop the skills that helped make it happen.

Katie brought a mature workflow to the process that was more than just the ability to upload clips, sequence images, add some music, and insert transitions. From our earliest glimpses into her work, Katie knew how to do these things for effect. Partially, this was due to her using what were arguably more sophisticated tools. However, her involvement in the community of YouTubers who actively explored the craft of creating visual compositions had a far greater impact.

Additionally, Jack was able to merge the work of the IC project with the National Writing Project's efforts in the area of Common Core State Standards and the Literacy Design Collaborative (LDC). The LDC task bank aided in purposefully aligning the standards to the task that students would be pursuing. By using the template provided by the LDC, we reworked the project to be more specific in its focus on addressing CCSS W.8.1 related to argument writing (Literacy Design Collaborative, 2014).

By more closely aligning the work of the IC project to the CCSS, students were asked to pay careful attention to the research process, take into account the opposing viewpoint, and actively take a stand in debunking this point of view.

This is something that flows throughout Katie's piece as she works to avoid platitudes and connect with her audience in a meaningful way. Because of the transformative nature of moving from research writing to making a more structured, multimedia public service announcement (PSA), Katie engaged in the writing process as she continually refined her piece from a more traditional research paper into a multimedia argument related to the issue that was researched. This created a real-world pathway for Katie to bridge the authentic work she was doing in her outside life with the artificiality that Katie associated with her school world.

Students were also asked to think about their work in close relationship to the actual community in which they lived. This requirement added elements of Connected Learning, as students were not only operating in a production-centered way. This newly CCSS-aligned module asked students to participate in the openly networked environment of their school and community and to reach out to experts in the areas that they were studying. Katie connected with a high school guidance counselor who introduced her to some of the support that is available in the community for people struggling with alcohol abuse. As we turn at this point to look more closely at Katie's work and the realizations of her journey as a digital creator, it would be helpful to pause and watch the video itself on the Digital Is website, if not already viewed.

Katie's audience was her peer group, and her goal was to approach this piece with the attitude that alcohol problems exist in our community, and we cannot stick our heads in the sand and ignore them. That is what led to the first draft, with a message that was not well-positioned for an 8th-grade audience. In her first draft, she asked students to remember to not drink too much at parties. Her message missed the mark for middle school students. But it was not completely invalid. She realized that 8th-grade students were only months from high school and could soon be in these situations. Her final piece is the result of considerable revision on her part and careful contemplation of her audience and intended message.

As we viewed her work again through the Collaborative Assessment Protocol, we began to wonder about some of the elements of this work that we might have overlooked. We knew that many of the decisions and moves that Katie made within the work could be informative in helping shape this work for future students. We came to understand Katie's process and her work in a new and informative way (see Figure 4.1).

Sometimes simplicity is powerful. From the first few frames of her piece, Katie establishes a clear motif as a creator in the way that she presents her words, voice, images, music, and ideas.

The use of white text on a changing but subtle background keeps the focus on the words themselves. The voice-over provides an audible version of the same text that is on the screen. Though this could create monotony by just repeating what is already obviously present in the words on the screen, it is the careful way that she reads the words and the tone of her voice that serve to further enforce the importance of these words. The vocal work in the section from 0:15–0:23 seconds shows how she is carefully using her speech to convey her intended emotion.

Figure 4.1. Images from Katie's Video

A: Initial screenshot from Katie's video (0:01–0:05)

B: Screenshot of the accident (0:34)

C: Short video clip of "Jackie Moon" character promoting alcohol from the movie *Semi-Pro* (Alterman, 2008) (0:58)

D: Image of Cookie Monster and additional costumed character (2:49)

E: Image of a boyfriend whispering "I love you . . . " (2:53)
[image blurred to avoid right violation]

Initially, her voice is well-paced and audibly compassionate as she allows her words to settle and affect the audience. Later, she allows it to raise into a question when prompting the audience about why they should care about the issue of teen alcohol abuse. At 0:28 seconds, as the text continues to offer insights into the teen alcohol abuse problem, Katie chooses to add extra echo to the voice-over track. Though this is a small touch, it catches the audience off-guard and re-engages us in the piece. It is these small changes in pacing and effects that keep her work from getting bogged down in the simple recitation of text on the screen. At its simplest, Katie is just reading text from the screen, but the decisions she makes about how to read the text go a long way to further her message and to draw the audience deeper into the substance of her very powerful message.

As the text interplays with Katie's voice on the screen, the other very present element is the soundtrack to this piece. The light, instrumental music is something that does not dominate the audience's attention, but is subtle and infectious at the same time. It is a song that many people are familiar with, and after a few moments viewers find themselves singing the lyrics in the back of their mind as they watch and listen to the message being delivered. The song "Mad World," a remake of a Tears for Fears 1983 song (Jules, 2006), is well-suited for the message of the piece. As we hum the lyrics in the back of our mind, it is obvious that Katie is pointing out the very real problems of our "mad world" as she tries to communicate to her peers about this complicated issue.

While some of her words move across a black background, others float across a video clip that works to further enhance the meaning of her words. It is the balance between stark white text on a black background and text over video clips that keeps the audience engaged as she reads the text on the screen.

As she sets the table for the difficult message of her piece, Katie shows us a crowd of people walking (see Figure 4.1a). The perspective makes us feel as if we are in that crowd working with these people. At this moment, very early in the work, Katie brings her audience in and reminds us that we are all in this together while at the same time providing the harsh reality of the statistics through text on the screen and her spoken words.

The video clip of the car accident at 0:34 seconds serves to startle the audience and scream out loudly about the urgency of the problem (see Figure 4.1b). Later, the video clip of Jackie Moon is used to lighten the mood (see Figure 4.1c). This clip highlights society's obses-sion with alcohol and allows the audience to stay engaged in the piece without feeling completely emotionally exhausted. This is a powerful moment in the work, and it is something that is instantly familiar to the students who compose her audience.

At this 0:54 marker, the topic could start to wear further on the audience and cause a middle school student to start to drift away. This clip is Katie communicating directly to her audience. She is saying that she knows they do not want someone to be preachy to them. She is showing them that she is one of them. In this moment of ethos, Katie is able to make her audience laugh and then remind them that this is something that is worth their consideration from a source that they can relate to. She continues to create an us-against-them posi-tion as she explores the idea of the vast advertising that kids are ex-posed to. Katie has an awareness that young people are bombarded with advertisements for alcohol, and she takes this opportunity to show this to her peers who might not have given it much thought in the past. This is a moment where she builds the bond with her au-dience that she will ultimately lean on as she makes her case against alcohol abuse.

In her adult audience, this is a moment of pause as we realize that this young digital composer is pointing out the very real problem that is created for young people by the alcohol and advertising industries. Here both the adult and student audiences are offered a look at what Katie is trying to combat. Not only is she attempting to convey to her audience the dangers of alcohol abuse, but she also is holding up a mirror to show some of the root cause of this larger problem. Katie continues to use words and music to get this point across until the 2:15 time marker.

This marks a turning point in the video. During the creation pro-cess, there was a lot of conversation about what should happen at this juncture. This appears to be a very natural ending point for the work. Two minutes is a comfortable amount of time for her message, and she has given her audience a lot to consider.

Katie the digital artist was not without her lines in the sand. When she shared her revised piece with her IC team and us, most people in the room felt that this was the place to bring the piece to a close. However, Katie wanted to end on a more positive note. By using the *seize the day* message from *Dead Poets Society*, she hoped to create an inspirational moment. Ultimately, Katie was the creator and we all respected her decision.

Continuing through a series of funny and light clips on friendship, Katie is bringing us to one more dramatic moment. She follows these light feelings with the thought that a victim of alcohol abuse could one day be your own child. This cleverly crafted roller-coaster ride of emotions is well-paced and gets the audience to the end of her piece when she firmly positions herself on the side of her peers and asks them to "try" to follow her advice, again reiterating her less threatening and didactic message.

Most of what we see on television is very preachy. It tells kids to "Just Say No" and to be better than the temptations that they may face. But if you have ever been a teenager, you quickly learn that this is often easy to say but difficult to do. In her work, Katie tries to avoid some of the eye-rolling that she might have anticipated by positioning herself on the same side as the students in her audience. She is one of them. She wants them to know that she "gets it" but at the same time provide a real connection between herself and her peers. By focusing on the relationships between friends and loved ones, she is attempting to leverage this emotion to create a connection around her message. This demonstrates her commitment to the vision that she had for the PSA (persistence, creativity).

At the end of the day, the message that her piece ultimately conveys pushes the boundaries for middle school. However edgy the piece might seem, it speaks in the authentic voice of a young woman who has friends not much older than herself dealing with the issues of alcohol abuse. While her final product remains edgy and avoids many common PSA clichés, it represents her carefully honed message through a deliberate and thoughtful use of the writing process. Many of the clips that are present in the piece are nods to her classmates and the memes of the day, inside jokes that most audience members in her age bracket would instantly recognize. For example, the boyfriend in Figure 4.1e who spins with the camera was a popular video that was sent among kids who were trying to show they were really into a new girl they were dating. While still making her point about the impact that destructive decisions can have on the people we love, she is able to connect with her audience. It is these moments that give her message the credibility that an outsider from the adult world does not have. She is one of them and speaking to them.

IMPLICATIONS FOR INSTRUCTION AND ASSESSMENT

When considering Katie as a creator of digital media, she is clearly on her way to becoming a technical master—someone who had lots of experience composing digitally with a purposeful vision for her work in her earliest drafts. For this inquiry project, Katie, the artist, wanted to showcase her considerable skills, with the content secondary at first.

As Daniel Pink describes in his book *Drive*, autonomy, mastery, and purpose are key components of a Type I person (2011). As someone who did not achieve great academic success, Katie flourished under the conditions established for this project, and her autonomy, mastery, and purpose were on full display. These were habits of mind that she had not previously applied to her academic life, but rather had reserved for her own personal work, where she was able to function in a more sophisticated manner, even if it is not one that conforms to the confines of middle school academia.

As Katie created her piece, she took several key steps that moved her work beyond the realm of the traditional research paper. It is obvious that she is not reading from an essay text as she narrates her PSA. Essentially, what she was able to do was take the key ideas from her paper and reimagine them with the tools that she now had available to her. Not all of her factual research had to be used directly. Of course, some of the research is brought to the audience through her narration, but just as much is brought through her use of images, music, and video clips that convey the striking, impactful message that she is trying to convey to her audience.

Katie's work, like many of the IC projects, aimed to speak to its audience in an authentic voice. For some students this meant connecting with school counselors and other agencies in the town through interviews and surveys; and for others, it meant engaging in email exchanges with people from outside of the state.

Katie's early draft highlights the fact that though her work may be visually and technically impressive, it is still the content of the piece that had to take center stage. As we evaluate rich student work, we are keeping the content learning at the center. This speaks to the concerns of many "content" area teachers who hesitate to dive too deeply into authentic literacy experiences. The "stuff" of the piece still must remain central to the focus of our work with students.

The focus on high-stakes testing at Dover Schools and most schools around the country doesn't seem to hold a sense of urgency with many students like Katie, who are more interested in using technology to create and to learn in the world. For Katie, opportunities to publish her work to authentic audiences is what motivates her to continue to hone her skills beyond the test and her grade level and, ultimately, school as it exists today.

> The "test" doesn't come close to capturing what our kids need to know and to be able to do at this moment of rapid and radical change, and . . . the longer we wait to start a conversation around doing school "differently," instead of simply "better," the more we're putting our kids at risk. All of this is, in many ways, a tough sell. (Richardson, 2012, Kindle Locations 81–83)

EPILOGUE

Like any small town, Dover is a great place with a close-knit feeling of community. The middle/high school complex serves as the center of town, with most important local events occurring in either the gym or auditorium, or on the track and field complex. Of course, the town has problems, and like much of America, drug and alcohol abuse is chief among them. Students in the 8th grade are at the transitional moment when they will move from being sheltered, innocent children to teens who will experience many of the darker realities of life.

A few months ago Katie, now a 10th-grader, met with us to revisit her 8th-grade PSA and share her matured reflections. As we watched her piece together, she bristled at some of her voice-overs and laughed at her titling techniques, no longer "cool" enough for a 10th-grader, but she remained adamant that including the "seize the day" segment from *Dead Poets Society* added power to her piece. We applauded her artistic license, and as the video ended and Katie looked up at us, we all agreed that her 8th-grade work still held its own. She was proud of her work.

As she talked about her current school projects, she reflected, "I still make videos for class. But now we have lists of what to include and how many pictures and stuff are needed. I can put that together quick. It's easier, but not important." Yet out of school she was excited to share that she and Amanda, another member of her 8th-grade tech team, were collaborating on new projects. They had brainstormed ideas, written notes on the ideas, and then crossed stuff out and whit-ed stuff out—a really messy notebook.

Her sharing and receiving of feedback was still fueling her passion to continue her ongoing work in the digital world. She didn't need an A awarded by a teacher. She had what she needed to move forward. The critical 21st-century tool for success—collaboration—was now something she sought out.

> Just imagine the learners they could become if we made these skills the focus of our work; if, instead of passing the test, we made those ever-more important skills of networking, inquiry, creation, sharing, unlearning, and relearning the answer to the "why school" question. (Richardson, 2012, Kindle Locations 601–603)

CHAPTER 5

Chocolate and Change
Gaming for Social Justice

Christina Puntel
Philadelphia Writing Project (Pennsylvania)

digitalis.nwp.org/resource/6272

Welcome to Parkway Northwest High School for Peace and Social Justice, Philadelphia, PA! This small public school was reimagined as a school for peace and justice through a community effort in 2005. According to Elliott Seif (2009) in an article in *Educational Leadership*, this effort "enhanced the culture of the school; gave students opportunities to reflect on their own values, beliefs, and behaviors; offered enriched academic learning experiences; and encouraged students to serve others." The library was often abuzz with researchers. Students, crowding around computers, books, and magazines, became researchers in order to teach others what they were learning. The student center, with a college student to act as the "guide on the side," was a force in cocreating curriculum and developing leadership capacity for peace and social justice in our students and staff.

As a school, we practiced a model of a collaborative teaching environment in a program we called SHARE (Spanish, History, Art, Research, and English). SHARE celebrated and supported student-led teach-ins and workshops with the support of our school librarian and many teachers. My involvement in SHARE grew out of a strong desire on my part to get away from overuse of worksheets and prepackaged curricula. As a school, we came together in SHARE to strengthen our college preparatory curriculum, involving 9th-graders in college-level discourse and research while employing sophomores, juniors, and seniors in mixed-grade groups to develop leadership skills. As a staff, we were well aware that students were entering college, but the statistics about how many students finished college were not as clear. In 2010 a report issued by the School District of Philadelphia using data from the National Student Clearinghouse suggested that just one out of 10 students who entered a public high school as a freshman in 1999 earned a degree from a 2- or 4-year college 10 years later (Mezzacappa, 2010). Some of us on the staff decided that in order to prepare students for college, we should engage in college-level work, read college-level texts, and treat all students as if they were researchers from the moment they entered our doors.

In 2014, we have no librarian, no student center, and our computers, while much loved and cared for, have all seen better days. Our school lost numerous research tools essential to a college preparatory school. The SHARE model (with the central goal of students learning to teach others) unraveled. Facing these losses at our school and, indeed, the erosion of public education in Philadelphia forced me to focus on my values. I believe in the power of education for peace and social justice. As a young teacher, I learned firsthand from teachers in the Philadelphia Teachers' Learning Cooperative what happens when you provision your class with rich materials that keep natural curiosity alive. While the budget scenario in Philadelphia is draconian at best, as a class we used our imagination and creativity to "resist together the obstacles that prevent the flowering of our joy" (Freire, 1997/2013, p. 69). We continued to work in the room that used to be the library. We talked about what kinds of environments encourage deep research and rich composition. We did not use the budget as an excuse. At the same time, we did not excuse the politicians who made these lasting scars on the face of Philadelphia's public school system. Thinking globally gave us the power to reach out to educate one another about issues that were even more dire than what we were confronted with every day.

Thus, even in the face of funding inequality, we encourage one another as teachers to integrate themes of social responsibility into academics. We are often invited to teach a course that reflects the values of our peace and justice school. Though I am the full-time Spanish teacher, I was invited to teach a class for freshmen called Multicultural Ethical Issues. We began the course with a close reading of Martin

Luther King's "Christmas Sermon on Peace to Ebenezer Baptist Church" (1967), with a focus on this part:

> It really boils down to this: that all life is interrelated. We are all caught in an inescapable network of mutuality, tied into a single garment of destiny. Whatever affects one directly, affects all indirectly. We are made to live together because of the interrelated structure of reality. Did you ever stop to think that you can't leave for your job in the morning without being dependent on most of the world? You get up in the morning and go to the bathroom and reach over for the sponge, and that's handed to you by a Pacific islander. You reach for a bar of soap, and that's given to you at the hands of a Frenchman. And then you go into the kitchen to drink your coffee for the morning, and that's poured into your cup by a South American. And maybe you want tea: that's poured into your cup by a Chinese. Or maybe you're desirous of having cocoa for breakfast, and that's poured into your cup by a West African. And then you reach over for your toast, and that's given to you at the hands of an English-speaking farmer, not to mention the baker. And before you finish eating breakfast in the morning, you've depended on more than half of the world. This is the way our universe is structured, this is its interrelated quality. We aren't going to have peace on earth until we recognize this basic fact of the interrelated structure of all reality.

Together, we explored issues of access to water, food, education, good work, and peace, always with the goal of educating others about these issues and taking some action together as a class toward creating a better world for all of us. After I shared my research about these issues with my students, they were encouraged to do further research and create teach-ins or conferences for their peers around these issues.

As Paulo Freire (1997/2013) writes in *Pedagogy of Freedom*, "There is a relationship between the joy essential to teaching activity and hope. Hope is something shared between teachers and students. The hope that we can learn together, teach together, be curiously impatient together, produce something together, and resist together the obstacles that prevent the flowering of our joy" (p. 69). The Multicultural Ethical Issues course was not about memorizing the problems we face as humans on this amazing planet, but instead creating knowledge that could be shared with others, and eventually changing the world.

When I am teaching something new in my Spanish classes or in the Multicultural Ethical Issues class, I sit up on a stool and use the

SmartBoard to zoom in and out of the content, encouraging conversation, listening, reading, and writing. Students know they will see these words again on the test, and take notes on their phones or in their notebooks from me. When we are composing, the classroom becomes more of a liminal space. In their book *Inside Out: Strategies for Teaching Writing,* Dawn Latta Kirby and Darren Crovitz (2012) describe a *liminal space* as one where "typical power relationships between people are temporarily set aside in an effort to encourage fellowship, honesty, and understanding. Liminal spaces are spaces of change, growth and shifting meanings, with potential rewards for those venturing into them" (p. 49).

In our "liminal space," we research together. We might watch a documentary and problematize what we've seen in classroom discussions. We read articles and chapters of books on the same theme. We do text renderings together. We write. Then it is time to share what we know with others during a teach-in. This is when students might create found poetry from the movie, choreograph a dance based on a section of the documentary, or make dolls to represent different people and their stories from the film and unit of study. The classroom comes alive with student work, student voices, and student research.

DESCRIBING THE PROJECT: THE TEACH-IN

As part of the Multicultural Ethical Issues course, we held teach-ins for other students at Parkway Northwest two times during the semester. For one unit, I used chocolate to explore questions about child labor, education, trade, and consumerism. I researched on my own about the United Nations' Millennium Development Goals (MDGs) as well as organizations that were working toward these goals, like Oxfam. Oxfam is an international group devoted to partnership with organizations and individuals to end poverty in innovative ways. The MDGs, shown in Figure 5.1, are eight goals, adopted at the Millennium Summit in September 2000, that encouraged the global community to address the world's main challenges to development with a target date of 2015 (United Nations, 2008; www.un.org/millenniumgoals/).

No matter how good this kind of learning is, how much it invigorated my teaching and upped my game when it came to composing digitally for social justice, it was not easy to pull it off with such a paucity of resources. With these disastrous budget cuts as a backdrop,

Figure 5.1. The United Nations' Eight Millennium Development Goals

Source: United Nations, 2008; www.un.org/millenniumgoals/

I tried to take what I had learned from SHARE about the power of research and reciprocal teaching, and applied it on a smaller level in my class. I worked hard to make my own research processes as transparent as possible, while also engaging students in myriad ways to experience, explore, and research further about these peace and justice issues.

In an article for the National Writing Project's publication, *The Quarterly*, the author of *Reading, Writing, and Rising Up*, Linda Christensen (2000), writes, "Students need opportunities to think deeply about other people—why they do what they do, why they think what they think. They also need chances to care about each other and the world" (Bigelow & Christensen, 2001). As I was teaching the course, I constantly encouraged students to find powerful tools that would work to educate their peers about the relationship between our role as chocolate consumers and global poverty (see Figure 5.2 for my instructions for a teach-in). In order to teach others, creating a worksheet just does not work. PowerPoint can be overused and sometimes feels like just another way to create lecture-style lessons. Powerful tools might include:

Figure 5.2. Christina's Instructions for the Teach-In

Teach-in Project

We will host a workshop for other classes at Parkway Northwest High School. In this workshop, we want your peers to analyze the role we play as consumers in the global marketplace, especially how our spending decisions impact others. You will create an active, hands-on presentation, and invite your peers to take actions about the cocoa trade. You will guide participants in a learning experience you design for them. You can this any way you want, except you may not use PowerPoint.

As part of your learning experience, you should also include some action that your peers can take to make a better world. Your peers should walk away with an increased awareness about the role of consumers in social justice issues.

- Creating an interactive textbook chapter
- Developing a photojournal
- Composing a short film
- Making a game

In regard to accomplishing the Millennium Development Goals, students felt that raising awareness about fair-trade cocoa and farming cooperatives and the role of women and children, as well as education and health care issues, would encourage their peers to be aware of their role and change their position from mindless consumer toward mindfulness and action. In the end, the teach-in was all about caring about each other and the world.

The way students chose to present their teach-in was always just that: a choice. This choice was also part of a high-stakes assessment of their learning in my course. How would their peers react to their presentations? How successful would they be at inspiring their peers to take action about these issues? How many people would they get to sign their petition, or write a letter to the company asking for better working conditions for their workers, or ask for fair-trade products from their local markets? Students often were expert at pinpointing effective media to reach their peers. What was my role as the teacher?

If you walked into my classroom during the preparations for these miniconferences, the air would be buzzing; our liminal space was *alive*! Students were choreographing in the halls, the drama group was rehearsing, students were busy researching, while others huddled around a piece of paper writing outlines for their group rap. My role in those moments was one of a conductor of an orchestra, a connector, a catalyst: "Try this website. Look at the work of this filmmaker. You might want to check out GoAnimate (goanimate.com) to make that come alive. Focus on this part, let the rest go."

As I walked around the room visiting groups in the throes of deciding how to share their research, I noticed Brandon and Tre looking perplexed. I'd seen these two in the library at lunchtime, listening to music and hunched over the computers. I didn't know them very well. I knew Brandon attended a Tech Camp at a local community organization and that he had way more experience creating digital work than I. When I met with them, they both were at a loss about how to share their research about the perils of child labor in the chocolate industry as well as the promise of fair trade and local cooperatives. Around this time, I had just watched Jane McGonigal's (2010) TED talk about how gaming can make a better world. "Do either of you know anything about how to make games?" I asked. Tre could work in Scratch (scratch.mit.edu). Brandon wanted to show us a website he'd started playing around with at his Tech Camp that summer. It was called GameStar Mechanic (gamestarmechanic.com).

At home, I live with two serious gamers. As a teacher, I became inspired by students in my classes who also devoted their time outside school to gaming. Jim Gee, a pioneer in gamifying the classroom and author of the book *What Video Games Have to Teach Us About Learning and Literacy* (2003), also lays out a wonderful, very accessible framework about how video games teach in an article in Huffington Post (2011). Gee writes that "gamers have to think like designers even to play, since they have to figure out how the 'rule system' in the game works and how it can be used to accomplish their goals. They can go further and 'mod' the game (make new levels or versions) by using the design software by which the game was made" (Gee, 2011). For Brandon and Tre, as well as other students in my Multicultural Ethical Issues course, games offered a powerful teaching tool for their peers. Further, creating a video game about the perils of the cocoa trade allowed two serious gamers, Brandon and Tre, to develop a message for their peers about the promise of fair trade.

I didn't know anything about GameStar Mechanic at the time, and found out from Brandon that it was a closed community, built on the idea that you can learn how to build video games by playing games, gaining different building skills through different activities.

Brandon talked about the balance of video games: "They can't be too hard or they are impossible to play. Too much frustration is not good." I asked them to listen to Jane McGonigal's (2010) TED talk before they began designing the game, and checked in with them periodically. McGonigal begins her talk so powerfully: "I'm Jane McGonigal. I'm a game designer . . . My goal for the next decade is to try to make it as easy to save the world in real life as it is to save the world in online games." In discussions that followed, we talked about whether we really believed gaming could change the world. Tre was not so sure. Brandon wasn't either. They played games for lots of reasons, and none of them was to save the world. As I watched them work, I knew something awesome was happening, but anytime teachers allow for a great deal of student choice, it's always hard to know exactly what is going to happen.

To complete their game, Brandon had to finish his training in GameStar Mechanic. He did this in school and at home. Tre was the research arm of the duo, checking facts about cocoa farming, child labor, and fair trade. In *Confronting the Challenges of Participatory Culture: Media Education for the 21st Century,* Henry Jenkins (2009) describes the work of "participatory cultures," where collective intelligence and socially distributed cognition arise between people as they collaborate to solve problems. For Brandon and Tre, this participatory culture afforded them the chance to create together without relying on one person for all of the information they needed to get the job done. Brandon and Tre showed that we can know more and do more together with the right tools. Neither student needed to know everything about how to conduct the research, check source credibility, produce the argument, and develop the game, but they were able to collaborate effectively. In the end, Brandon called himself the "creator" and Tre called himself the "tester." As an observer, I saw both of them deeply engaged in the process and would say they developed the game together.

In a very short time (students have 2 weeks to put together their teach-ins), Cocoa Thief emerged as a powerful teaching tool. When time came for the workshops, I could only scrounge two laptops for their table, so not many of their peers could play the game at once. Cocoa Thief was created by Brandon and Tre to educate their peers about the perils of the cocoa industry and the promise of fair trade (see Figure 5.3).

Still, the crowd around their table was electric. Students stayed to watch and play, trying to beat the game, asking questions about how they created it, and signing a fair-trade pledge that Tre and Brandon

Figure 5.3. Cocoa Thief Start Page

Google and the Google logo are registered trademarks of Google Inc., used with permission. "Cocoa Thief" used by permission of E-Line Media.

prepared for their classmates (see Figure 5.4). This pledge came from their reading and research on a campaign launched by Global Exchange, an international human rights group dedicated to social, economic, and environmental justice around the globe.

Figure 5.4. Brandon and Tre's Fair-Trade Pledge

FAIR TRADE PLEDGE

_____'s Fair Trade purchases and actions will change lives for farmers and villages who grow cocoa. More education! Less child slavery!

I/we resolve to take action this month (check all that apply):

__ Talk about Fair Trade chocolate with friends
__ Ask stores where I shop to go Fair Trade
__ Look for Fair Trade symbols on my chocolate
__ Buy Fair Trade Chocolate

Date pledge made: _____

Signature: _____

Adapted from Global Exchange Fair Trade Pledge.

Brandon and Tre both put hours of their time in school and out of school to create the game, play the game, and then make a walk-through for their game. As I looked back on their work together, their game, and their research, it was obvious they successfully completed the assignment. They engaged their peers by designing a game that re-created the feeling of working in the cocoa industry, with all of the dangers from overseers with weapons on the farm to dangerous factory conditions in cocoa-processing facilities. They talked up a solution: fair trade.

Brandon and Tre's project was part of many experiences during the teach-ins. In the end, the teach-in included the following projects:

- A cypher (group rap)
- A GoAnimate cartoon
- A choreographed dance
- A chocolate tasting and role-play

The variety of experiences allowed their peers many different touch-points during the teach-ins, ensuring that every student came away with a full picture of the complexities of the cocoa industry and our place in it.

As a high school teacher, assessing work like this is complicated by our numerical grading system. I use teacher-made rubrics to assign a number grade, as I did in this project. Did you hand in your research with citations? (10 points). Did you create a fact sheet about your topic, answering at least five questions to pull your research together? (10 points). Did you finish your presentation on time? (10 points). Did you have an "action" for your peers to take that correlated to your research? (10 points). Still, this rubric cannot get at the intricacies of creating these learning experiences and does not adequately express the complexities involved in creating digital work like a video game. How could I look at their work to gain an understanding of these many layers?

INSIGHTS FROM THE PROCESS

I entered into the process of looking deeply at the video game and the walkthrough with my colleagues with many other experiences of using the Descriptive Review Process behind me. In Philadelphia, teachers from the Philadelphia Teachers' Learning Cooperative (PTLC) have been meeting in one another's' homes for almost 40 years to describe work using the Prospect Processes developed by Patricia Carini and others. Along with these processes, PTLC strengthened my values around student choice, play, making, and collaboration. Centering my teaching in these values and processes has taught me to value the strengths of my students, to see them in their works, and to use these strengths to guide my teaching (Carini, 2001). Further, I learned about the power of oral inquiry processes to bring about change and equity as I gathered with colleagues from around my city to describe work from students of all ages. By focusing on one child, we speak back to top-down, blanket reform solutions (Abu El-Haj, 2003).

The stance that I learned from engaging in processes like the Descriptive Review of Work and the Descriptive Review of Practice (Himley, Strieb, Carini, Kanevsky, & Wice, 2011) gives me unlimited space to move around in as a teacher. I am not bound by what the student can't do. I am not hung up on what they need to learn. My teaching does not draw on a finite set of standards to guide my practice. Instead, through these oral inquiry processes, I can see the child's standards in the work. I come to know the student through the work. I can see the possibilities.

Through the Descriptive Review Process, Brandon and Tre's work came alive for me. In order to describe the work, I had Brandon and Tre create a video game walkthrough for their game, Cocoa Thief. The game was hard to play for adults who are not avid gamers and who don't have the time to learn the timing to beat the game. Brandon and Tre have clearly studied the walkthrough genre, because theirs was up there with the most informative I've heard. They used QuickTime to create a screencast—a recording of themselves talking while showing the computer screen, clicking through various elements of the game—and shared their walkthrough on YouTube. Walkthroughs, cheats, playthroughs, FAQs, and codes are tools gamers create to share with others to show how to play the game, highlight hidden elements, share surprises, and more. Gamers create them in many ways, written and with video. The walkthrough takes the audience through the game step by step. They are usually compiled on sites like YouTube (youtube.com) and GameFAQs (gamefaqs.com) and easily referred to when you get stuck in a game, or if you just want to see how someone else solved a particular problem. The idea to have Brandon and Tre make the walkthrough was purely for the audience of my peers, so that when we engaged in the Descriptive Review of the game, we would get to see as much of it as possible. Turns out, creating walk-throughs is a perfect way to encourage the metacognitive work so at the heart of the Framework for Success in Post Secondary Writing (CWPA et al., 2011).

After Brandon and Tre made their walkthrough, it was obvious that the game itself was one text and that the walkthrough was anoth-er text. Each serves a different purpose. The game allowed their peers to enter into the world of a worker on a cocoa plantation, with all its perils. In the walkthrough, the creators of the video game explained their thinking about the social justice issues as well as details about how the game itself was created, the timing, and the level of difficulty.

Learning from My Colleagues: Engaging in the Descriptive Review Process

In the first part of the Descriptive Review, my colleagues shared what they saw/noticed in the video game that Tre and Brandon created, as well as in their walkthrough.

As I listened, I began to see different facets of the game and walk-through emerge through the inquiry process. The game, which can be shared with others online, is a quest game with a 5-minute time limit. It has a title, Cocoa Thief. The directions tell the user what controls to use in order to collect cocoa beans, avoid overseers (snipers!), and escape the field. My colleagues shared how they saw a postcolonial society represented in the game. The inequities of society were re-flected in the difficulty level of the game. The game was hard to play! My colleagues noted how the creators demonstrated a procedural un-derstanding of the cocoa industry, from farm to factory. As the round continued, describing the design of the game from the visuals to the sound opened me up to see how Brandon and Tre reflected the duality present in cocoa production (see Figure 5.5). Each scene of the game presents a different aspect of cocoa production. Information bubbles popped up (where exclamation marks appeared on the screen) to in-terrupt play and give the player information about the cocoa trade, from field to factory.

What's working in the piece? As we continued with the Descrip-tive Review, I listened as my colleagues described what worked in the piece. By purposefully looking at what works, we rise against

Figure 5.5. Screenshots from the Cocoa Thief Game Demonstrating Concepts Related to Fair Trade

A: Opening Scene from
the Cocoa Thief Game

Here, the duality of the lushness of the cocoa plants as well as the hardships and hazards for those harvesting the pods remind the player of the perils inherent in the cocoa industry.

B: Encountering an
Injured Worker

Given the limited availability of characters in the game, here a mummy represents an injured worker that the player encounters. The speech bubble of the "injured worker" reads: "*sigh* My animals and my crops are going to be taken away."

C: Question from
the Main Character

In this speech bubble, the game's main character (played by the gamer) asks another character in the game, "Are you protected with Fair Trade?"

the prevailing winds that assess student work through the lens of deficiency.

Brandon and Tre were valued as game-makers, researchers, and collaborators for social justice. In the walkthrough, one of my colleagues pointed out that Brandon says, "It's all about patience," the patience needed to create the game, develop the characters, and make it playable.

The design of the game also worked for the audience. The use of different blocks (forest, industrial) as well as the familiar design made it visually appealing. My colleagues noted that since the game was hard, they had to interact with it over and over and over again. The fact that it was hard meant they had to take time out to play. This brought forth a sense of shared understanding. One colleague shared that games are motivating and engaging for students. She found herself getting very excited each time she made a little bit more progress.

Brandon and Tre came alive in the work as the conversation continued. I realized that I was seeing them in a new light. When I grade work in class, I very rarely feel close to a student, or gain deep insight into them as makers, designers, workers for peace and justice. Through this process, I saw Brandon for the first time as someone who worked hard to produce a very complex game, with Tre as lead researcher and tester. Since the game is built very effectively on the basic conventions of a quest, this led me to wonder how much time both students have spent playing, reading, and generally interacting with the quest game genre. Further, I realized how complicated the game must have been to put together. Neither student does much talking during group discussion or even in small groups. This game let me see the hard work they put into creating a tool that talks for them.

Brandon and Tre are also not highly interactive in class. Tre is great at keeping pace with me during instruction or in small groups, and Brandon might lift his head from his notebook once or twice during a class, but neither are highly interactive. However, my colleagues pointed out that the interactivity needed to get better at the game over time worked as a way to engage in learning the content and think about social justice issues. Another colleague suggested that for a teacher and a parent, the embedded meaning works: "My child and my students could learn something from a game that is fun to play." As one colleague pointed out, games are just "cool ways" to share knowledge, experience, and understanding.

The game was fun to play, but, as I mentioned before, it was hard. One of my colleagues who understood the workings of GameStar Mechanic pointed out that "balance is one of the notions of GameStar Mechanic—student is playing with that notion of balance and thinking through how hard it can be in terms of reaching the tipping point." Brandon spent some time trying to explain this notion to me as they were creating the game. When my colleague noticed this concept, it validated Brandon's process. This also made Tre's role in the creation of the game (testing, playing, revising, offering suggestions) equally vital.

What questions does this piece inspire? Finally, my colleagues shared their questions about the game itself and the screencast describing it (see Figure 5.6). The screencast walkthrough that Brandon and Tre created ended up inspiring me to use this format for other projects, as a way for students to reflect on their work.

Figure 5.6. Cocoa Thief Demo on YouTube

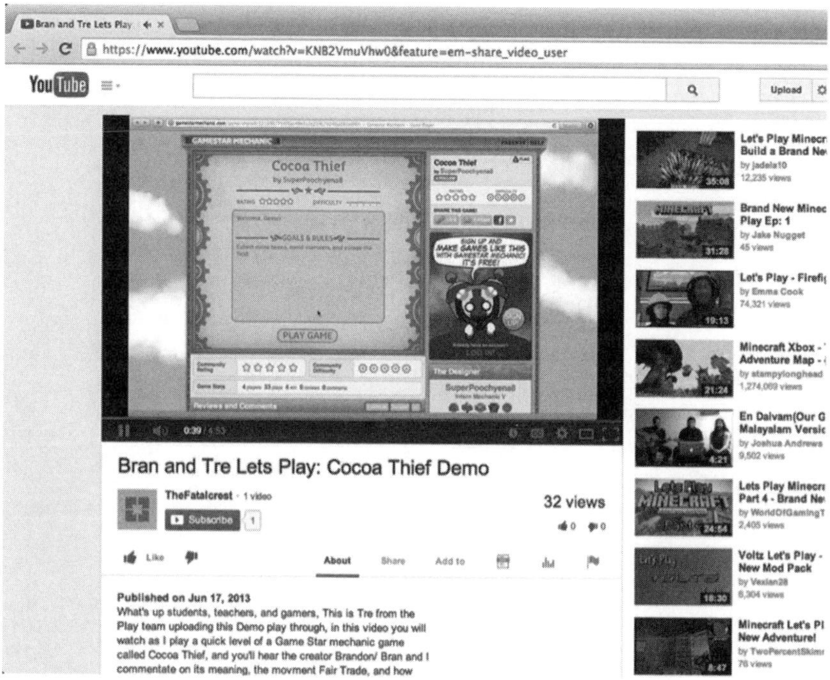

Google and the Google logo are registered trademarks of Google Inc., used with permission. "Cocoa Thief" used by permission of E-Line Media.

This round provided me with many places to go next with my teaching and learning. In summarizing this round of the process, I noticed questions centered around the content (fair trade), the process (creating a game and a walkthrough), and connectedness (how can others play this game? how can others learn about fair trade?). As we engaged in this round, questions emerged about the issue of fair trade: How well did the students really understand this concept? How did I know students understood the cocoa trade? Is there some kind of scaffolding the students could give to people like me (and maybe their parents?) who want to learn more about how to play the game successfully? And what about fair trade? These questions brought up some key points for me. Brandon and Tre's game was part of a larger workshop that featured many digital compositions about social justice and consumerism. While these two students may not have all the information about fair trade to 100% accuracy, the class's knowledge-making together expressed a very full picture of how buying fair trade positively impacts farmers and their communities. In fact, this called to mind the CCSS ELA Literacy Standard that asks students to "initiate and participate effectively in a range of collaborative discussions (one-on-one, in groups, and teacher-led) with diverse partners on grades 11–12 topics, texts, and issues, building on others' ideas and expressing their own clearly and persuasively" (CCSS.ELA-Literacy. SL.11-12.4, corestandards.org/ELA-Literacy/SL/11-12/4/).

As a teacher, I value the power of the entire Multicultural Ethical Issues class to express this knowledge together. I also value the individual student's ability to "present information, findings, and supporting evidence, conveying a clear and distinct perspective, such that listeners can follow the line of reasoning, alternative or opposing perspectives are addressed, and the organization, development, substance, and style are appropriate to purpose, audience, and a range of formal and informal tasks" (CCSS.ELA-Literacy.SL.11-12.4, corestandards. org/ELA-Literacy/SL/11-12/4/). This set of questions helped me think about ways I might have students provide scaffolding to their audience in order to clarify their own thinking about the issue or topic.

Throughout this round, we discussed the power of games and the power of walkthroughs (screencasts) in learning. Games need to be played over and over. Playing them over and over allows us to become steeped in the creator's world. This is different from composing for the page in some ways. But it's also similar to the way we go back over and over again to favorite books and poems and reread them. The Framework for Success in Post-Secondary Writing high-lights metacognition as a vital habit of mind for college readiness. So often, digital work in my class is rushed. With the popularity of Vine (vine.com) with its 6-second videos that loop and other short media, I struggle to find ways students can reflect on their work. Screencasting in QuickTime (or with the SnagIt Chrome extension) to make a walk-through provides a structure to talk through the digital work, expand on details, and let the audience in on the process used to create the piece.

Implications for Instruction and Assessment

Role of the teacher. Reflecting on the process, I realize no rubric could have captured the many angles through which my colleagues and I looked at the game Brandon and Tre created. As I encourage these students and the others I teach in Multicultural Ethical Issues classes or in my own Spanish classes, I continue to value the stance the Descriptive Review Process affords me. Whether I gather with teachers to look at student work in person or online, the power of oral inquiry gives me insight into the student's strengths as well as ideas for further works, different methods, and expanding my role as teacher and learner. During this process, I was also introduced to the Multimodal Assessment Project from NWP (MAP, 2013). When students compose digitally in my classroom, sometimes I have a hard time encouraging next steps and revision in the works they create. This framework gives me some tools to help scaffold those processes, while still valuing student choice. I am particularly excited about two of the domains, "substance" and "process management and technical skills," in this framework as I plan further projects and themes.

In terms of process, my colleagues' questions about how long students had, what criteria they were given, and what drafting this game looked like helped me see just how much time Brandon and Tre put into the game, both at school and at home. These students had their own criteria for the game (hard, but not too hard). Further, they knew that the game had to teach others about the perils of the cocoa trade and the promise of fair trade. Process questions from my colleagues about composing the game (Is there a way to make the icons/char-acters clearer to the user? Who are they? Who do they represent? What is their role?) gave me some places to go in my own practice with these students and their game as well as other students and their digital compositions. During these student-led projects, my role can be one that pushes students to explain their work, to define their characters for the audience, and to produce explanations embedded in their work. Questions like, "I wonder if he will build additional levels?" and even "I wonder if there is something that the characters can do together that they can't do alone?" further helped me focus my role. Many times, I find myself marveling at the elaborate digital work my students create and have a hard time seeing where I might challenge them to rework and revise.

Going deeper and connecting more. The NWP's work with Multimodal Assessment further clarified how I might challenge my students to revise their work around the domain they call "substance." As I work with students, I want the substance of the digital piece to pack a punch. As I design further projects, I will use the language of the framework with them to get at what makes substance stand out in their work. This conversation encouraged me to think about the way I might conference with students during the composing to pose questions about genre and characters, and encourage them to go deeper.

While going deeper is certainly a goal of future work, I also want to think about how to connect work. In terms of the game, colleagues asked questions wondering why there were no comments on the game from the GameStar community, asking what the feedback is like from the online community, and how many students played the game the day of the workshop. I realized that I had a great deal to learn about how to make the work of my students connected. Just composing online does not ensure connectedness. How can I rethink the ways we share our multimodal compositions within our school community and with other communities in our city and beyond?

The Descriptive Review of Brandon and Tre's game helped me see where I can expand my role as teacher as students compose digitally and by hand to ensure that the complex messages of the work reach the audience in all of its nuance. The screencast is quickly becoming a vital tool as I encourage students to go deeper and connect their work with others. No budget cuts can hold us back as we compose digitally for social justice in these liminal spaces. Students' digital creations are powerful tools as we think globally and act locally here in Philadelphia. Look out for more young people like Brandon and Tre who will change the world one game at a time.

CHAPTER 6

Remix and Remediate
Social Composing for More Than Just the Web

Stephanie West-Puckett

Tar River Writing Project (North Carolina)

digitalis.nwp.org/resource/6281

THIS I BELIEVE ABOUT TEACHING WRITING

One of the most difficult challenges of teaching 1st-year writing at the university level is moving students from a set of tightly held, prescriptive beliefs about what constitutes good writing into a space where they can broadly consider the unique rhetorical situation of every composition. Each semester, multiple students tell me they've never written anything for school other than a five-paragraph essay, and they look at me incredulously when I tell them that their thesis might not be best located in the last sentence of their first paragraph. They tell me good writers put five to seven sentences in every paragraph and never use contractions, and I tell them that this semester we're going to break all those rules and write with more than words on a page or a screen, just to see what might happen.

According to the Framework for Success in Postsecondary Writing (CWPA et al., 2011), successful postsecondary writers should cultivate eight habits of mind: creativity, curiosity, openness, engagement, flexibility, metacognition, persistence, and responsibility. These habits, according to the Council of Writing Program Administrators, National Council of Teachers of English, and National Writing Project, can be fostered in classrooms that foreground critical and rhetorical thinking, help students pay attention to writing processes and develop knowledge of disciplinary and genre conventions, and encourage students to compose texts in both traditional and new media environments. As a 1st-year composition instructor at a regional public university, I work to seed these behaviors and orientations by giving students in my classes a wide range of choices about the texts that they create, access to and support for a variety of digital composition tools and composing heuristics, and perhaps most importantly the freedom to try new and difficult projects by untangling project failure from course failure.

A couple of semesters ago, the incoming freshmen in the Jarvis Leadership Program, a new living and learning community at East Carolina University, were asked to read essays in the book *This I Believe: The Personal Philosophies of Remarkable Men and Women* (Allison & Gediman, 2007), which they would discuss in their freshman seminar, a course meant to better prepare them for the demands of college life. As I was teaching two sections of English 1100 specially flagged for these Jarvis Leadership cohorts, I wanted to capitalize on this common read and designed a multimodal project around the wildly popular This I Believe (TIB) phenomenon that asked students to compose at the intersections of image, word, and sound. Like most teachers who pick up this kind of project, I asked students to communicate a strongly held belief to a public, perhaps their peers here on campus. I asked that they find strategies to communicate their beliefs that were fresh and interesting, complex and unexpected. I communicated that the belief should make their audience think deeply and differently about the topic they chose to explore.

Since I use a contract approach to grading that evaluates students' composing behaviors as opposed to students' composed products (Danielewicz & Elbow, 2009), students did not receive rubrics or other tools that defined assessment measures for the TIB project. Unlike more traditional grading systems that place value on a student's performance or a student's ability to produce an ideal text that the instructor has outlined in a rubric, contract grading systems privilege the behaviors that strong writers engage in, linking behaviors, not written products, to specific grades. In my classroom, those behaviors are closely aligned to the Framework for Success in Postsecondary Writing as well as the Writing Program Administrators' *Outcomes Statement for First-Year Composition* (CWPA, 2008), and I made the move away from grading individual products to make my emphasis on process, risk-taking, and reflection more tangible to students. Inspired by Brannon and Knoblauch's (1982) dated but still relevant "On Students' Rights to Their Own Texts," the contract grading approach, while frustrating for student writers who are accustomed to prescriptive and formulaic writing instruction, returns textual ownership to composers and constructs them as responsible agents who create texts that enact their aims and purposes, not mine (see Figure 6.1 for my grading contract).

Since their course assessment is holistically measured, our in-class discussions are focused on naming, practicing, and reflecting on the behaviors that strong writers engage in, and considering how those behaviors might look on the screen and in the room over the course of the project. During the This I Believe discussions, I stressed that their evaluations were based on their sustained involvement in each stage of the writing process from planning and drafting, to soliciting and revising with both peer and instructor feedback, to publishing and reflecting thoughtfully on their composing processes and products. I underscored the importance of embracing creativity and responsibility. I asked that they respect the deadlines, as I believe a community of writers should be encouraged to both wander off into their own creative fields and to convene regularly, bearing witness to the struggles to make meaning while circulating good ideas, strategies, and approaches to a particular project.

To start, students were required to find and analyze three TIB examples, each representing a different medium, to read like a writer by using mentor texts. Students curated and analyzed several different kinds of TIB texts including podcasts embedded on websites containing essay texts and accompanying images, print-based essays in their course textbook, digital stories with still photos and spoken text on YouTube, and animations that told stories through drawings and motions with few words and sometimes loud soundtracks. We engaged in rich in-class discussions about the conventions of TIB, noticing the ways writers used experience-based narratives as evidence for particular beliefs and considering the macro- and micro-level moves that these writers were making to construct powerful snapshot moments to convey their experiences. We also considered the processes of remix and remediation that we were seeing across media, considering how multimodal TIB composers used sounds and images as powerful story elements, combining new and existing media as ways of situating themselves and their bodies and making meaning in particular times and places.

Figure 6.1. Contract Grading Requirements for the Course

Grading

This course uses a contract approach to grading. The contract approach privileges the behaviors (listed below) that strong writers engage in, linking behaviors, not written products, to specific grades. Simply put, if you take this class experience seriously, challenge yourself to make learning stretches, and pay close, careful attention to your writing and to the writing of others, your composition skills, confidence, and success will grow.

You are graded on the following course expectations:

1. attending class, on time, with all necessary materials every class period and participating fully in all exercises and activities, both face-to-face and in virtual spaces;

2. meeting due dates (you must ask for a deadline extension in writing prior to the assignment due date if you are experiencing extreme circumstances) and fulfilling reading and writing criteria (including word count requirements) for all formal and informal writing and reading assignments;

3. discovering significant questions to consider and address via writing;

4. exploring the many different purposes of writing, including writing to reflect, analyze, explain, and persuade;

5. increasing your awareness of organizational strategies and your ability to apply them and becoming attentive to how audience and purpose affect content, tone, and style;

6. incorporating sufficient and appropriate details and examples both from your experiences and from secondary research;

7. expressing your ideas with clarity and with effective syntax and punctuation;

8. engaging in ambitious, thoughtful, mature projects that demonstrate a complexity of thought and sustained effort and investment on each draft of all assignments and making substantive revisions to two major projects—extending or changing the thinking or organization—not just editing or touching up;

9. giving thoughtful, substantial, well-articulated feedback to peers during class workshops both face-to-face & virtually;

10. submitting all assignments for peer and instructor review, demonstrating thoughtful reflection on those assignments by identifying your rhetorical context and discussing and evaluating the writing strategies that you've chosen to fulfill the demands of the rhetorical situation, and submitting your final e-portfolio to your instructor by the deadline.

Students then composed a design plan that explored preliminary choices for their own TIB compositions and worked to articulate an understanding of their audiences, purposes, contexts, media, strategies, and arrangements, a rhetorical approach to multimodal composition that Wysocki and Lynch (2007) outline in *Compose, Design, Advocate*. While I've always believed that if we want students to engage deeply in assignments, we should encourage them to choose their own topics for writing and inquiry, I've also come to see the value in having students take responsibility for choosing other parameters of their compositions, particularly audiences, contexts, strategies, and media. Harkening back to Brannon and Knoblauch, this focus on choice throughout their writing processes opens up the composing field to more diverse textual processes and products and encourages students to assume responsibility for all of the major features of their texts, not just topic selection.

Once they had sketched out some of their preliminary choices for the TIB project, students shared their design plans with their peers, and I provided feedback as well, pushing them to articulate more clearly or to provide more detail about a particular section. Almost always, students struggle here with applying a sense of context, and I prompt them to think about how they are situating their compositions alongside or against other texts and cultural practices, asking them to consider what relationships their composition will have to the larger social order. Over the course of the semester, they become more savvy in thinking through the material consequences of their compositions, but this line of thinking is largely new to them as many haven't been asked to consider webs of socially produced meaning and the extradiscursive impacts of their own writing.

We discussed Selber's (2004) heuristic that outlines the functional, critical, and rhetorical areas of digital literacy, and we made support groups into which students self-selected to provide targeted support for peers in that particular area where they felt they had some degree of expertise. Then, four 75-minute class periods were devoted to the composing and peer support processes. Some students used time to complete tutorials on programs like iMovie, Windows Movie Maker, Photoshop, Podcastomatic (podcastomatic.com), SoundCloud (soundcloud.com), or GarageBand. Many more just jumped into their program of choice and began to play, starting first to haphazardly incorporate photos, videos, or sound. I encouraged them to tack far and near with respect to their design plans, using them as guides but also being willing to stray from them if they discovered an approach or a serendipitous moment in their composing processes. I also noticed that some students were using this time mainly to watch others, to observe how others negotiated all these choices.

This is one reason I really like to have students compose with new media in the classroom. The materiality of the remixed objects—the songs, the images, the oversized words on a screen—allows students to see and hear composing practices in a new way, to find entry points where they can meaningfully and constructively intervene in one another's composing processes and create shared meanings around their products. All too often, I think, writing teachers fall back on peer review activities that focus students' attention on surface features of texts, asking students to critique and evaluate late drafts, drafts that are near completion. This is not surprising considering alpha linguistic text production is largely invisible until a writer has strung enough words, sentences, and paragraphs together to make a draft. But by that point, student writers are often wedded to those words. And naturally so, as it takes a good deal of labor to produce a text. They often resist bringing others, particularly their peers, into the composing process, as they are likely to "undo" and perhaps devalue all the hard work of drafting.

Multimedia composing activities make the tools and processes of writing more transparent; words, images, icons, videos, and other elements all combine in a visual manner from the very beginning of the composing process. Thus students have more opportunities to intervene earlier in one another's writing processes, working as engaged coproducers, even during invention stages, where bits of texts, galleries of images, strings of video clips, and stacks of audio tracks are audible, visible, and more tangible as building blocks of meaning-making. In addition, these kinds of digitally produced texts are easily shared and circulated, and they are more likely to be "used" rather than just "read." As we know from cultural studies, objects-in-use bind communities and create recursive relationships among makers and users, and this is no different from textual or digital objects like the podcast, the YouTube video, or the digital story. Through multimodal and multimediated digital writing, I am able to more quickly create social composing space that provides both tools and access to distributed knowledges about writing. While this is certainly possible with more traditional texts, multimodal and multimediated writing kick-starts this process and sets up powerful communal writing relationships that students can draw on when the writing becomes more textual and less transparent.

So while lurking is certainly an entry point to participating in a community, I began, during the second week of in-class composing, to worry about this handful of students actively and intently watching others but not returning to their own work. I couldn't see their texts developing in the room, and I was concerned that they would have nothing to share as the deadline for a "tentatively stable" draft was quickly approaching. I had read and responded to their design plans and knew their emerging ideas, but I wanted to see their composing work happening, to be a part of it. I love nothing more than engaging as another cocreator in the writing classroom (Haswell, 2006), helping students materialize their texts, so finally I broached the subject. "I'm still getting ideas," one student said. "It's too chaotic and cramped in here for me," another reported.

"It's the lighting," Zeke said. "I've noticed too much variation of natural light from the windows, and I need consistent artificial brightness to pull this off. Don't worry, Ms. W-P. You're going to love this."

NARRATING A STORY OF FORGIVENESS

This is the story of Zeke's TIB stop-motion animation titled "Forgiveness-1ZR," a 2 minute and 36 second video available on YouTube (Reep, 2012; see youtube.com/watch?v=22N1gGapvts) with over 100 views, a text *in circulation*, at the time of this book's publication. On the day that completed drafts were due for peer review in class, Ezekiel—Zeke—was eager to share his piece. "Not with Hannah, though," he said. "She's seen it all—frame by frame." Hannah proceeded to tell me that she and Zeke had spent hours together in the dorm the night before completing their TIB drafts and had, together, taken over 750 still-image frames to complete their stop-motion videos.

"It's done," Zeke said.

"For now," I replied.

Zeke's video begins with a loud instrumental electronic soundtrack characterized by discordant synthesizers and high-octave notes that sound like they are played on a xylophone. On the screen, line drawings of superheroes loom in the background while a disembodied hand places a Krispy Kreme coffee mug down on a flat, nondescript surface. Out of the mug emerges a two-dimensional figure with a hole in his head similar to a doughnut (Figure 6.2a). The angle then shifts, and we see the mug recede while a toy truck with monster wheels rolls in the foreground. Then the coffee mug advances and the figure climbs to the edge of the rim and sits, teetering for a few seconds before falling off. He is caught by an extended hand, and we get a quick, almost subliminal, down shot of the author, wearing a sleeveless shirt, sitting in a chair in what appears to be a dorm room (Figure 6.2b).

The human picks up the figure with the other hand and places him on a dry-erase board. The figure seems to squirm for a few frames, and then the hand picks up a dry-erase marker. In the background, there are framed photographs of a family that come in and out of view with each frame (Figure 6.2c). The hand removes the cap of the Expo marker and appears to redraw the figure. Then the word "Boom" appears in the bottom right corner of the dry-erase board. This explosion propels the figure to the bottom center of the board. The figure raises his hand and speech bubbles begin to appear in quick succession. "One idea can stop a war" (Figure 6.2d). "One idea can heal the soul." "One idea can bring peace." Then we see the speech bubble as it is erased and there is a pause.

Next, phrases appear in the speech bubble that eventually read, "On May 15, 2012, my father made the decision to LEAVE." The pacing here is slower as three underlines show up under the word "leave" and we again see the erasure of the words, with "leave" being the last to disappear. In similar fashion the words "He left his wife, two daughters, and two sons" appear and are erased. The next speech bubble contains four periods and then morphs into a broken instead of a solid line while the picture of the family we saw in the background earlier materializes inside the bubble. The solid lines appear, constructing the bubble again, and we read the text, "We were . . ." and then "hurt," "broken," "confused," and "sad." Behind the word sad, a frowny face appears. The speech bubble now disappears and the word "My" is followed by a symbolic drawing of Earth with the word "world" appearing gradually, one letter at a time, along the top curve with the words "fell apart" below (Figure 6.2e).

The board is shown half-erased and the figure returns again with another speech bubble that eventually reads, "Summer was HARD," then "I spent most of it," and finally "ANGRY." The figure then moves to the bottom center of the board and the words "Flash" and "Forward" appear large in two successive screens. A star similar to the comic "Pow!" commonplace grows and seems to explode. Next a horizon

Figure 6.2. Sequential Screenshots from Zeke's Video

line and a rock appear at the bottom of the dry-erase board. The figure sits on the rock and fidgets while three thought bubbles extend up to the left of the board. A question mark appears in the largest bubble. Then the words "Now I'm in college" appear one by one. Then again, word by word, "And my dad came back!" appears (Figure 6.2f). A small speech bubble beside the figure reads, "hmm . . ." and then the figure walks to the other side of the board.

Suddenly, the board is flipped from a horizontal to a vertical orientation and the figure is shown from waist up in close proximity to the camera. The thought bubbles again rise and the figure disappears as the bubble is filled with these words appearing in sequence: "I've softened my heart . . ." The word "softened" is underlined before the word "my" appears. Next the words, also in sequence: "I've decided to," appear, and the word "forgive," is spelled out letter by letter in a large font (Figure 6.2g). All of the letters in the bubble are erased, and the words "and forget" are spelled out with "forget" in the large font like "forgive." Everything on the board disappears except the word "forget." Then the "get" is erased and replaced with "give." The word "forgiven" appears and is erased then the words, "This I Know" appear. "Know" is erased and replaced with the word "believe" spelled out letter by letter. The next few frames show the words "This is an E.S. Reep Production," and a smiling face with teeth appears at the bottom of the board. The figure is then shown one last time with a speech bubble that slowly spells out "bye" (Figure 6.2h). The last frames roll a credit sequence that includes "Story and Photos by Ezekiel Reep" and a music credit for Adam Kroll's song "Emigrant," remixed from the free music archive. The words scroll offscreen, and the music fades out.

Zeke's classmates were mesmerized. His peer reviewer quickly called others over to see the video once it had started, and nearly the entire class was watching. He received a great deal of unscripted, authentic praise for this video, and it was clear that he thoroughly enjoyed the compliments and accolades. Later, during his peer review session, Zeke thoughtfully asked and answered questions, taking notes, at times, on what his reviewer said. I asked him about the long intro, wondering if he might shorten it, and asked him to consider the timing on some of the frames, as a couple of people in class said that they didn't read that fast. Zeke responded that he thought his audience needed the long introduction to get used to the style of the piece and identify with his figure and that he didn't intend to change the pacing, as he wanted some parts to be barely graspable. "If you need to watch it again to get it all," he said, "you can. It's only like 2 minutes."

A week or so later when the final pieces were due, Zeke's composition had not changed since the original draft that he had shared with the class. In his reflection on the piece (see sirezekiel.wordpress.com/2012/11/29/peer-response-essay), he discussed the ways that "I have been twisted, scrutinized, stretched, and eventually applauded for my work in Jarvis English 1100." He writes that reading, listening to, and watching others' projects that reflected on their relationships with their parents inspired him to take on this piece, and once he knew what he wanted to do, "a total of 4 hours was spent creating my video and I was quite impressed with the results, as were my instructor and classmates." There was no doubt that he recognized our sincere and emotional reactions to this piece, and those were what stayed with him, even in the final course evaluations.

While Zeke's product is clearly a strong example of a multimodal TIB project, one of those student pieces that I have returned to long after the semester is over, Zeke's behaviors presented a problem for the grading contract that I use in my classes. First, Zeke did not show commitment to revision, making substantive changes on each additional draft, as is stressed in the contract. He produced a first cut that got the emotional response he was looking for, and that was enough for him. Second, Zeke's reflective response didn't provide a great deal of detail about his composing practices. I assume he used edited images to create the line-drawn effects at the beginning of the video and dry-erase drawings for the rest, snapping photos that he then loaded into Windows Movie Maker, but I'm not sure. Zeke's inability to make his composing processes transparent here frustrates me; I fear his lack of clarity reinforces the myth of mysterious writing muse who imparts knowledge from above, not from within. It also ignores the contributions made among members of a community, struggling to make, share, and communicate meaning with particular tools at particular times in particular places.

I know from his previous work in class that he is an illustrator, and the reflection piece mentions that this was his first experience using "Windows Movie Maker and cameras." He doesn't reflect on his rhetorical choices, nor does he evaluate the video and its impact on intended audiences beyond recognizing the "wow factor." When I asked him about the absence of this kind of careful reflection, he shrugged and said he'd laid out a careful plan that he thought he'd executed well. When I looked back at his plan, however, it wasn't that well-developed, and I assume the brunt of planning, composing, and revising work of this piece happened in the serendipitous moment that brought together a fine illustrator, a well-told story, the right tools, the right environment, a good peer support system, and, of course, a fast-approaching deadline. This moment is surely one that can produce a powerful composition, but does that production mean that the student fully engaged in the material and intellectual work of college composition?

ASKING CRITICAL QUESTIONS ABOUT DIGITAL COMPOSING

Seeing this artifact through the eyes of my colleagues helped me conceptualize both what was and what was not there in Zeke's composition. As the Multimodal Assessment Project outlines, each artifact is part and parcel of its context; however, taking this piece out of its context helped me to look at it from new angles, to consider the substance of the piece and the "artifact's message in relationship to the contextual elements of purpose, genre, and audiences" (MAP Group, 2013). Because this video has so many nuanced layers and complementary modes at work in each frame, my understanding of the piece benefited from having seven pairs of eyes and ears cataloging the video's elements and our editor's careful documentation of our discussion.

During the noticing element of the protocol, several teachers pointed out the author's use of genre conventions that are part of both comic books and graphic novels. They noticed the comic characters, specifically Batman, in the first few frames; Zeke's straight-edged hand-lettering that made use of mixed cases and underlining; and particularly, the use of the four main types of speech bubbles commonly employed in graphic forms. Some commented on the balance of text and images, and one teacher said that the piece felt like a graphic novel in motion with all the "visual fun" that one expects in a graphic form. As someone who never learned to read comic books and has almost no knowledge of graphic conventions, these comments helped me see the forms that the author was playing with, forms that his audience was likely more aware of than I.

Another common theme that my colleagues noticed was the brevity and minimalism of Zeke's story. As colleague stated,

There is a lot left unsaid—the author made a lot of different choices and did not tell us exactly why his dad left—that choice allowed me lots of space to imagine what happened and wonder about the father and the story. That sense of wonder happened at other points, too, like the part where he describes going away to college. There were lots of places for the audience to experience it as we wanted to.

This comment made me realize that his classmates and I had already read a version of this story much earlier that semester, a version that was primarily text-based and developed the moment of his father's leaving in greater detail. Zeke and I had discussed the emotional power of that early piece, and during the protocol, I began to understand that his classmates and I had a rich backstory that my colleagues conducting the protocol did not. "Forgiveness Version 1.0," the text-based form, however, was about his mother's love, courage, and forgiveness during this emotional time, and his tone toward his father was neutral. Version 2.0, the video artifact described here, is, I think, a continuation of that story. Zeke assumes his audience's familiarity with the story; therefore, he briefly recaps the moment of leaving, focuses more on his emotional response, and moves the story forward to show his audience a change of heart and how that has helped him develop a strongly held belief in the power of forgiveness. My colleague's comment above sparked a remembering that helped me see how Zeke was, perhaps, considering his audience's background and familiarity with the topic and understand this rhetorical move as a choice to focus on the substance of forgiveness and the power of a firmly held belief.

Perhaps the most poignant comment one of my colleagues made while in the noticing stages of this piece was that "Forgiveness-1ZR" was a "well-constructed technical piece." As others had pointed out, this video demonstrated incredible craftsmanship and attention to detail—from the interactive camera angles to the carefully paced storytelling techniques that built anticipation and interpolation with the characters inside Zeke's story world. He had clearly worked to exploit the technical tools to produce the heavily filtered effects that were noted during the protocol, and his product demonstrates that he could create a storyboard in iMovie that integrated sounds, picture, and words; render that video in an appropriate file format; and upload the video to a YouTube channel to share with his audiences. His mastery of technical skill here is impressive, and we see that he can clearly use pens, computers, and cameras as tools to achieve end goals. His statement that he had executed his plan resonates here, and it also throws into relief Zeke's resistance to taking a critical stance about the technology itself and about the artifact he created with it.

When the protocol moved to addressing "what's working" in Zeke's piece, I found that my colleagues voiced many of my own evaluations. One teacher reported that she really liked the music, noting that it seemed to fit the tone and the tempo of the narrative. Another mentioned the layers of meaning-making the student was engaging in, stating, "Like an onion, or a Russian nesting doll, the shavings that were left behind got to another layer. We couldn't see a rock, but there was an idea of a rock building up over time—really worked and resonated." Still another mentioned the black-and-white color scheme as appropriate for his minimalist style.

A majority of the comments in this section of the protocol, however, focused on the pathos of the piece. My colleagues characterized the piece as emotive and self-referential, noting that rhetorical moves such as including the family photo helped them invest in the story. One teacher mentioned that through brevity and a keen sense of timing, Zeke had created an ethos of honesty that kept her interested and engaged. Others noted that the video surprised and confused them. The juxtaposition of language from global to specific in phrases like "I softened my heart" and "My world fell apart" was unexpected for one teacher, particularly when paired with the dissonance of the soundtrack. Another teacher was confused by the genre itself, wondering throughout the video, "What is this?," a question that she says is never really resolved even as the video pauses before looping again to the beginning.

For me, these comments echo those that Zeke heard in the room the day he shared his piece and make me believe that he did, indeed, achieve his purpose of intensely engaging others for a short time to share the emotional chaos that can result from others' acts in the world. We talked a great deal in class about how to show instead of tell your story, using Penny Kittle's (2008) section of narrative engagement in her book *Write Beside Them*. From my colleagues' comments in this section of the protocol, I think Zeke was able to move beyond the mantra of "show don't tell" to provide his audience an embodied experience of emotion, one that suspends the logics of reason privileged in academe and reclaims the pathos of composing that gets devalued in our rhetorical tradition after the Sophists.

As we moved into the last section of protocol response, I was again reminded how little I knew about Zeke's composing processes for this piece. My colleagues asked several questions about his experience of composing, questions about software, tools, and specific processes that he used. Because the work of this piece happened largely outside of the classroom and Zeke's reflective piece did little to illuminate those processes, I couldn't answer many of the questions. Similarly, I couldn't talk knowledgeably about his choices in arrangement. Our editor, Troy, who apologized for being the "wet blanket," noted that Zeke's story really started around the :40 mark and ended around 2:13, making him wonder about the long intros and outros and their effectiveness. Another colleague mentioned that the piece felt disjointed to her, like two compositions, as there was no text in the first part of the video or what Troy referred to as the long introduction. A couple of teachers asked about his drafting process as well, wondering about how the piece changed and how he was able to use peer and instructor feedback. As I mentioned earlier, this piece was a one-and-done composition, and Zeke did not effectively demonstrate that he could use others' feedback with, perhaps, the exception of Hannah, who worked closely with him in the dorm.

Some of my colleagues wondered about the assignment itself, whether or not this type of open-ended project was typical of my classes and college writing courses in general, and others wondered if the structure of the assignment may have constrained the text, as one teacher noted that Zeke's belief statement seemed forced, a move made to convince the instructor that the piece was, in fact, a This I Believe essay. This prompted another colleague to ask if the student accomplished the goals of the TIB project. My colleagues prompted me to give the piece a grade, and I reminded them that my contract approach to grading doesn't grade individual compositions, but focuses on behaviors. They pushed me to give it a grade, but I resisted, taking some time instead to think about the behaviors Zeke was or was not able to demonstrate, behaviors that are closely linked to those habits of mind for success in postsecondary writing.

While I do think that Zeke was able to explore his creativity to produce a powerful composition that engaged his audience for a particular purpose, I don't think he was effectively able to demonstrate awareness of his composing practices, nor did he demonstrate in this project that he could evaluate the effectiveness of his rhetorical choices, critically assessing his product. In terms of Selber's (2004) constructions of digital literacy, Zeke seems to have demonstrated strong functional literacies, almost no critical literacy, and a rhetorical literacy that articulates an emerging understanding of the rhetorical situation (audience, purpose, and context) but doesn't account for the ways that his medium, strategy, and arrangement have impacted particular audiences. His sense of responsibility for the project was underdeveloped, and ultimately he was satisfied with a first draft, showing little persistence in his composing and drafting processes.

Another colleague wondered how Zeke viewed his project in relation to his classmates' projects. He noted that there was a certain amount of interest-driven learning that was occurring as students choose topics, tools, and modes for this project. Zeke does mention in his reflection that he was inspired by his classmates' stories that wrestled with complicated relationships with their parents, and his classmate Hannah also chose to focus her story around her father, who had helped her develop a belief in tattoos as a mode of visual self-expression, but he never compares his product to other products in the class or those he analyzed as mentor texts. Both Zeke's and Hannah's in-class comments indicated that they had helped each other during the process, and I think this is an important indication of the kinds of interest-driven and peer-supported work, albeit limited, that made their projects possible.

Interest-driven and peer-supported learning are two key features of the Connected Learning (CL) theory (Connected Learning Research Network, 2013). CL outlines both design and learning principles for helping young people grow and become creative and connected citizens in a digital age, and links together three essential elements for transformative learning: interest-driven, peer-supported, and academically oriented. In addition, CL outlines core properties of transformative learning environments that include production-centered activities such as making, experimenting, producing, and writing; open digital platforms that allow a learner to access resources in multiple settings; and shared purposes that link older and younger generations (see Figure 6.3, connectedlearning.tv/infographic). These principles, many of which seem intuitive in a digital writing workshop, have informed my practice and given me research-based justifications for much of the freedom and flexibility I design into projects such as the TIB project. And while the project is certainly academically oriented, it reveals some of the challenges that teachers can face when they embrace student culture and value interest-driven and peer-supported work in an

Figure 6.3. Visual Representation of the Connected Learning Model

Source: Connected Learning Research Network and Digital Media & Learning Research Hub

Creative Commons License: This Connected Learning Infographic is licensed under a Creative Commons Attribution 3.0 Unported License (connectedlearning.tv/infographic#cclicense).

academic setting. The next section will explore some of those challenges, picking up on the important "takeaways" I gained from the collaborative assessment conference discussion with my colleagues.

HOLDING ONTO SYNCRETIC TENSIONS
IN COMMUNITY AND COMPOSITION

Most of us have at least some familiarity with the concept of remix, a practice of invention defined by its use or "sampling" of existing work. Some argue that remix is the cultural glue of a read/ write generation (Lessig, 2008; Navas, 2006). As Stedman (2012) explores the concept, *remix* is a self-sponsored digital writing practice that happens organically in out-of-school spaces, most notably fan communities, where fans remix, remediate, mash up, and use techniques of assemblage or pastiche to create new texts that draw on the iconic symbols, characters, styles, audio tracks, and story worlds of their most beloved television shows, films, music books, songs, and video games. With deep roots in urban hip-hop music (Derecho, 2008), we can consider remix a culturally centered multimodal composing practice, one that lives most viably outside the classroom in popular and youth culture.

So what does it mean to bring this practice into the classroom as others have done (Banks, 2010; Dubisar & Palmeri, 2010; Stedman, 2012), and as I did with the This I Believe project? This is a question I wrestle with anytime I coopt and appropriate self-sponsored genres into the writing classroom. Each time I look at a student artifact, such as Zeke's video, this question comes into view differently, and I want to address it here through the lens of "Forgiveness-1ZR." This artifact clearly pays homage to Zeke's love of comics. As mentioned above, he uses several genre conventions that are part and parcel of the graphic form. He's sampled comic heroes as cultural icons, juxtaposing them with his own plain figure to give it a smaller-than-life appearance. He's borrowed comic elements such as the varied speech bubbles and the hand-lettered fonts to make meaning and create the "honesty" that one of my colleagues mentioned during the protocol. He's lifted a comic sense of perspective from the camera angles, creating visual interest and viewer disorientation. And it is this disorientation, I think, that propels the reader into Zeke's story world and creates an emotional response in his viewers. Zeke samples music from the free music archive and remixes family photos with line drawings, working to remediate the default modes of linguistic and aural production that we've come to association with This I Believe stories, making instead a graphic-heavy but textually and musically complemented This I Believe remix and remediation.

Clearly, Zeke came into my class with a wealth of cultural composing literacies, as do many of my students. Like Zeke, many produce powerful multimodal texts. And like Zeke, many are confused by their assessments, wondering why strong texts don't necessarily lead to strong evaluations. This simple relationship between good text and good grade is problematized in a classroom ecology like mine where awareness of social composing practices and developing rhetorical knowledge is valued over the production of a one-hit-wonder text. Many have called the 1st-year composition classroom a contact zone (Herrick, 2002; Pratt, 1991), as students from different backgrounds and cultures are asked to present their ways of knowing, doing, and being in the world and engage the same in others. As a teacher who works to recognize and value the literacies that students bring from their out-of-school experiences while developing the academic literacies that are necessary for success in college beyond the 1st year, my 1st-year writing classroom does feel like a contact zone, one where various cultural and academic literacies and rhetorics are always tenuously juxtaposed. This tension is made visible by Zeke's work and helps me understand both the affordances and the constraints of remixing the concept of remix itself in a university-level writing classroom.

Through the protocol, my colleagues helped me resee this artifact and rethink the 1st-year writing contact zone as a place where popular and academic writing practices can conflict as well as complement one another. As Gutiérrez (2008) argues, it important to acknowledge and hold these "syncretic tensions" if we want students to develop powerful literacies and rhetorical practices that can function in and outside of school. As a Connected Learning practitioner who believes that we learn best when that learning follows us from home to school to community setting, I will continue to adapt and appropriate cultural writing practices as ways to engage students and encourage creativity, and I will do so now with a more explicit focus on the habits of mind that foster persistence, responsibility, and metacognition.

Looking back through Zeke's text, I can see that he is not alone in his paucity of metacognitive work. I want each student to take the time to teach me about their forms and their unique composing processes, and I am dedicating more time to this work during class so that students know that it is valued. And while one of the tenants of my grading contract explicitly addresses reflecting deeply on both processes and products, most students coming from high-stakes testing environments have had little opportunity to build metacognitive capacities; thus I plan to address this more specifically in class, using mentor texts not just for projects like the TIB essay but also for the kinds of reflective writing that prompt us to be more rhetorically and critically aware social composers. From this rich professional development experience with my colleagues, I have begun to see that the work of teaching multimodal composing is a two-way street. Students have vast stores of cultural composing knowledge, but they need our help to make those knowledges visible and open them for reflection and critique. Only by engaging in those kinds of metacognitive activities around the production of text can they can become functional, critical, and rhetorical multimodal writers in the academy and beyond.

Conclusion

Troy Hicks

How do we effectively assess digital writing?

I have wrestled with this question since the publication of *The Digital Writing Workshop* (Hicks, 2009), in which I built the framework for the book on five components of workshop instruction: choice and inquiry, conferring, studying author's craft, publishing, and assessment.

In that book I first made the argument that "digital writing can be assessed, both formatively and summatively, and in smart ways" (p. 107). Relying on the MAPS heuristic—mode, media, audience, purpose, and situation—was one way to begin the assessment process as early as the assignment stage. Offering students specific insights into the expectations of the mode, or genre, as well as the particular media you might expect them to employ (such as text, images, or video), provides them with some criteria for the writing task. As I have been guilty of myself, and as Traci Gardner (2008) warns in her book *Designing Writing Assignments*:

> So much depends upon the writing assignments that we asked students to complete. . . . And yet, most of us have at one time or another presented students with an assignment designed at the last minute, moments before class starts. (p. x)

The same, I'm afraid, could also be said for assessments. While I can assure you that I did give considerable thought to the assessments described in *The Digital Writing Workshop*, one of my main strategies was to layer digital components onto existing assessment frameworks such as the Six Traits (Spandel, 2005). Much like Gardner warns, I look back now and think that perhaps I was trying to present something with that assessment that wasn't quite fully

119

formed in my own mind. I knew that many teachers were, and still are, familiar with the Six Traits, and so it made sense to think about moving them into the digital age. However, over the past 5 years, I've begun to think that this is part of an "old wine in new bottles" type of problem. I concluded, in 2009, that "trying to imagine new ways to assess digital writing while the tools and practices keep shifting under our feet is, at best, difficult" (p. 124). I stand by this statement; assessment still is tricky.

Thus, the present chapter attempts to accomplish two goals. First, to the extent that I'm able to do each of them justice, I want to acknowledge the work that my colleagues have done with their teacher research projects and explicitly discuss how they demonstrate qualities from the Multimodal Assessment Project, the Framework for Success in Postsecondary Writing, and the principles of Connected Learning, all the while connecting to the broader questions about digital writing assessment that have been raised by other teacher researchers and composition scholars.

Second, and perhaps more important, I want to provide concrete suggestions for how teachers can assess digital writing. Typically, this would be called a "theory to practice" section, or something similar. However, in the case of digital writing, no sooner do we wrap our heads around the way that students can present with one form of digital media when another pops up. We need theory, yes; however, it is the work of the seven teachers featured in this book—as well as dozens of others with whom I have worked over the past 5 years—that has truly informed my thinking about assessment of digital writing, and my hope is that I can summarize some of their insights in this final chapter. To do so, we must take an honest look at our assessment practices.

BROADENING OUR VISION OF ASSESSMENT

As noted throughout this book, and especially seen in conjunction with the use of the Collaborative Assessment Conference protocol, we as teachers are generally more likely to *evaluate* a piece of student work then we are to *assess* it. We pass judgment without being descriptive. This is evaluating, not assessing. Though not speaking of digital texts, in his collection *Alternatives to Grading Student Writing*, editor Stephen Tchudi (1997) argues:

Assessment asks broadly: "How did this project turn out?" "How is it turning out?" "Are you getting what you want from your audience?" "Can I suggest a few possibilities that might make this thing work better?" "What do you think your work needs?" "What are your ideas about how to make it more successful?" Assessment certainly incorporates reader response (to drafts as well as finished products), and it is often focused on practical, functional concerns: "What do I have to do to make this paper *work*?" (p. xiv)

Tchudi then goes on to contrast assessment and evaluation, noting that *"evaluation* implies fixed or a priori criteria rather than evolutionary or constructed values" (p. xv, emphasis in original).

Throughout this collection, we have seen examples of how these teacher researchers are thinking about these types of questions, layering in appropriate conversations about the nature and uses of digital media. We listened as Stephanie described her dilemma with Zeke because of contract grading (see Chapter 6), and we examine the ways in which Jeremy has changed the criteria for his book review project so students can gain deeper insights into how they will be assessed before they even begin (see Chapter 3). Also, given the types of feedback that are required to make a digital composition (and not just "a paper") work, could Aaron or Carson have succeeded in a classroom that did not value digital texts in the way that Erin's and Julie's did?

More recently, in *Writing Assessment and the Revolution in Digital Texts and Technologies*, Michael Neal (2010) has made his case for new ways of assessment:

We have this opportunity, while the texts and technologies are relatively new, to reframe our approaches to writing assessment so that they promote a rich and robust understanding of language and literacy. If we do not, we will follow the path to assessment technologies that was mapped out in the 20th century, in which assessment largely promoted reductive views of language in favor of the modernist agenda of efficiency, mechanization, and cost effectiveness. (p. 5)

We've noted throughout this collection how wonderfully complicated writing can become when it's opened up to various modes and media. For instance, is there any way that a computer could assess how Christina's students Brandon and Tre integrated their knowledge of the cocoa trade with the video game they constructed? Moreover, when they created the walkthrough video and discussed their compositional choices, is it possible to assign a score to every move they made as digital writers? Where is the rubric for that? The same types of questions could be asked for Katie's PSA that she created with Bonnie and Jack. The negotiations that they all engaged in led to a much richer project than any checklist or rubric alone could have provided.

And, returning to the quote that opened this collection, the National Writing Project's Multimodal Assessment Project Group has argued that in order to assess multimodal compositions, we "would need to go far beyond what conventional rubrics and assessment programs aim to touch" (MAP, 2013). How, then, can we go beyond? What is it that Tchudi and Neal—as well as countless others who have designed, analyzed, critiqued, and revised assessments—can tell us about the process of assessing multimodal projects?

First, the Multimodal Assessment Project reminds us that, "for any type of multimodal assessment to aid in learning, it needs the flexibility to address both the context and the developmental capacities of the learner" (MAP, 2013). While we may still designate particular criteria for the assessment, and the pressures of adhering to specific standards will only continue to increase in the era of the Common Core, we must understand that our digital writers are Connected Learners as well. Though we cannot allow them to choose every component of an assignment—mode, media, audience, purpose, and situation—we must allow them some autonomy given the incredible range of choices that they have available to them. Aaron, for example, may never have gotten to the deeper levels of understanding about monkeys had he simply ended his project with the basic written report. The heuristic provided by the Multimodal Assessment Project prompts us to remember the importance of context.

Next, from the Framework for Success, if it hadn't been clear enough already, our role as writing teacher has continued to evolve in the past decade such that we can no longer relegate our feedback to final drafts, nor can that feedback be solely intended to support a perfect product. From Shaughnessy's *Errors and Expectations* (1977) onward, countless writing teachers and researchers have claimed the necessity for guiding students through a writing process, and meta-analyses of research have confirmed the value of teaching and assessing from a process-oriented approach (Graham & Perin, 2007). However, the sad truth is that many of us have given lip service to teaching the process, conferring with students, and helping them develop drafts, reflect on revisions, and generally engage in the habits of mind promoted by the

Framework for Success. This must stop. We can no longer hide behind our own classroom doors and grading policies. Students are writing for a global audience, and whether we support them in that process, making it transparent and engaging in our writing classrooms, is up to us. The world judges our students on their writing, and we must take the old adage of "teaching the process" much more seriously, especially with the use of digital writing tools.

For instance, in thinking about one particular type of tool, bibliographic management software such as Endnote (endnote.com) or Zotero (zotero.org), there are multiple habits of mind that can be modeled and taught explicitly. First, as students search for sources, they can take responsibility for accurately documenting the texts that they encounter. Second, based on the type of project in which they are engaged, they can demonstrate persistence over the course of time as they continue to add related resources to their bibliography manager. Third, students can use their sources flexibly over an entire semester and throughout various projects. These are but three examples with one particular digital writing tool. Writing teachers who hope to engage their students in authentic research and truly teach the types of skills that are needed in college and beyond must embrace this kind of pedagogy.

Finally, from the Connected Learning framework, we recognize that digital writers have too many opportunities in front of them to waste their time on meaningless assignments. This is not to say that there is no way we can design assignments that will compete for their attention head-to-head with surfing the Internet or playing video games, because that is a specious argument. Everyone deserves some downtime, some distractions. Instead, the point I want to emphasize at the end of this collection is how the seven students represented in this collection had the opportunity to adapt their assignments around their own interests and felt continually supported in the process by their teachers as well as their peers. With the one exception of Zeke, who waited until the last moment to produce his piece of digital writing (and yet still relied on a classmate for help), all of the students in this book have demonstrated how participating in a broader learning network that extends beyond the classroom is an essential practice of digital writers.

These are complicated changes to keep in mind, mixed in with some uncomfortable truths about the ways in which writing has been taught for the past 3 decades. As I said above, we must change our practices, and we must do so now. With these ideas in mind, I now turn to three specific recommendations for teachers who want to move in new directions with digital writing assessment in their classrooms.

NEXT DIRECTIONS FOR DIGITAL WRITING ASSESSMENT

> Using these protocols with groups of teachers in our workshop series
> with student writing also provided teachers with a means of looking
> and talking about student work beyond mechanics. [It also provided]
> a means for students to look at the student work of their peers,
> taking more ownership for offering feedback and improving their own
> writing.
>
> —Bonnie Kaplan

In this final section, I offer three specific recommendations for teachers of digital writing to consider. Though I know that it will be nearly impossible to take up each of these suggestions in its idealized form, the experience that I've had working with Erin, Julie, Jeremy, Bonnie and Jack, Christina, and Stephanie has reminded me that a great deal is possible for teachers across school contexts, even when resources and technology appear to be scarce. We must become advocates for digital writing in much the same way that English teachers have historically advocated for students' rights to read all books without censorship. When our profession takes up a cause, we have the potential to initiate significant change inside the classroom as well as in our broader society. Teaching—and assessing—digital writing is a task that we, as professionals, must own before, as Michael Neal noted, it becomes mechanized. It is in this spirit that I offer the following recommendations.

Recommendation 1: We must acknowledge, accept, and defend the position that digital writing may not, in a causal and direct manner, improve students' achievement in traditional writing. Yet digital writing is still powerful, worthwhile learning.

> Going through the protocol impacted my teaching in ways I didn't
> expect. I realized as my colleagues asked me questions about Carson's
> process, I didn't know many of the answers. I knew that as I went into
> the next school year, I needed to build more student reflection into
> my instruction. I was more purposeful when immersing my students
> into digital mentors, noticing the moves authors made and the impact
> it had on their digital compositions. While conferring, I made it a
> point to ask students about the decisions they were making as they
> composed digitally. In addition, I asked students to share their thinking

with others in the class. As a result, they thought more carefully about their audience and purpose while composing. They were cognizant of the message they wanted to convey and made purposeful decisions about how to best get that message across. In the end, I could see a marked improvement in the work my students were doing.

—Julie Johnson

Upon first read, this particular recommendation may seem counter-intuitive. "Troy," you may ask, "don't we want to make the case that teaching digital writing is equally as important as teaching traditional writing?" On the one hand, yes, we certainly do want to make a case for balance and in some conversations making that argument may be sufficient. On the other hand, we also need to assess what Moran and Herrington (2013) describe as the "full context" for composing digital texts. That includes five components:

> the teachers' goals for student learning; the ways in which the teacher has positioned students; the full particulars of the assignment; a good sense of the dynamics and character of the classroom, whether face-to-face or online; and, from the samples of student work given, a good sense of the characters and capacities of the students. (last para.)

Sometimes this full context will include traditional and digital texts. Students may compose *both* a traditional text *and* a digital one, like Jeremy's book review project. Alternatively, students may compose a digital project *after* having completed other more traditional forms of academic writing, such as in Stephanie's classroom.

However, we must recognize that sophistication in digital writing may or may not have a causal, crossover effect on students' traditional writing skills. Despite the recent conversations among teachers and parents taking place online and in the popular media, this is not just a debate between cursive writing versus keyboarding. Rather, my point here is that we need to be honest with our students, colleagues, parents, and ourselves in the fact that not all digital writing skills will immediately translate into better academic essays. While we can coach and mentor students through the process, helping them identify the moves that all writers, including digital writers, make in effective compositions is difficult to do all the time.

For instance, Christina notes that her students Brandon and Tre were able to compose a fairly sophisticated video game while, more importantly, justifying their choices about the gameplay in light of what they learned about fair trade and cocoa farming. However, Christina is careful not to make a generalized claim about their improvement as essayists. Just because they made an argument through a video game, she does not say that they can necessarily write a thesis. Yet she didn't ask them to do this, either. In this particular case, she wanted them to feel free to create a digital composition without the typical requirements (and constraints) of an essay, noting that the audience and purpose for the school's teach-in presentations would be something quite different from trying to create an academic essay.

In practice, living with this dichotomy means that using digital writing in your classroom is defensible as a teaching position, but we need to be clear on the skills and standards we are aiming for with the digital writing task as it compares to (or layers on top of) traditional academic writing. It is appropriate, then, to have students engage in a variety of types of digital writing—from blogging to word processing, from creating digital videos to augmented reality projects—so long as we recognize that we are teaching in a mode of "both/and," not "either/or." Here are some specific ideas for doing so:

- While still explicitly teaching academic writing skills, such as organizational patterns in informational writing, how to create and defend a thesis in argument writing, and how to develop a narrative, provide students with opportunities to create both written academic texts and digital ones.
- When considering the skills that students will use, as well as your access to technology, work strategically to integrate digital literacies with academic writing. For instance, help students develop their own collections of academic resources using a bibliography manager and solicit feedback from their teachers and peers using the commenting and editing features of a word processor.
- As you develop assessment criteria for projects over the course of a unit, ask students themselves to name the skills and strategies that they are using with academic writing and connect them to what they are doing with their digital writing. What does it mean, for instance, to create a transition in an essay as compared to in a digital video? How are those thinking processes the same or different from one another?

Recommendation 2: When designing digital writing tasks, we must ask students to move beyond something that they could do without the affordances of digital tools. That is, the whole *must* be more than the sum of the parts.

One of the ways that this protocol has impacted my 8th-grade classroom is in how we look at our work. It seems obvious given the purpose of the protocol is to look at student work, but it has had a real impact on how we look at some of our more creative endeavors. When students are working with projects that are a bit outside the paradigm of the 5-paragraph essay, this protocol has proven very valuable. Whether students are examining book trailers they have crafted or critiquing their current progress on PSAs that they are creating, this protocol has given us a process and language to speak about our work in a way that goes past grades and numbers and letters and gets to the real core of what it means to be a creator and a critical partner. When working with this protocol on focusing on specific things they noticed or stating questions that the work raises for them, students are engaged in a level of conversation about their work that is powerful and definitely uniquely fostered by the protocol.

—Jack Zangerle

One substantive change that I have made with my teaching as a result of the collaborative assessment protocol is the way I have my students give feedback to each other through the revision process. Prior to going through the collaborative assessment protocol, I simply gave students a checklist of what they needed to check for on their peer's' papers. In addition, the students never had the opportunity to give positive feedback to their peers. For example, they didn't have the option to tell their classmates what they liked or what worked well for them as the reader or observer. As a result of going through the protocol on more than one occasion, I now create opportunities for my students to give more thoughtful, thorough feedback to their peers. As a result, I am seeing more polished writing and deeper conversations taking place among my students when it comes to the pieces that they compose for my class.

—Jeremy Hyler

In our article "No Longer a Luxury: Digital Literacy Can't Wait," Kristen Hawley Turner and I describe five ways that we can kill digital literacy in our classrooms, including a practice such as using blogs without blogging.

> Unfortunately, we see teachers using blogs in ways that do not capitalize on the conversational opportunities that blogging offers. One common practice that might kill students' digital literacy is a "call and response" blog where teachers post a question and students respond to that prompt, and ignore each other. Similar to the "initiate-respond-evaluate" patterns documented in classroom research, "call and response" blogs do not foster conversation or collaboration among students. They fail to develop digital literacy in meaningful ways. (Hicks & Turner, 2013, p. 60)

The problem, whether with blogs or any type of digital writing technology, is that we can often fall into traditional teaching patterns even when the digital tools present themselves as uniquely qualified for different purposes. An essay created with Google Docs, for instance, can easily be turned into a hyperlinked webpage with embedded images. The question is whether or not those hyperlinks and images enhance the meaning of the text.

So, in addition to some categories we would expect, such as organization, audience awareness, and appropriate use of details and examples, Wierszewski (2013) documents a variety of components unique to multimodal texts including creativity, movement, multimodality, and technical execution. Her study concludes:

> While this study demonstrates that teachers often borrow from print paradigms, it also indicates that teachers are actively generating concepts and criteria foreign to print essays as they respond to multimodal texts. Among these new kinds of comments are concepts like creativity and interaction between the modes, which reflect the goals of multimodal pedagogy outlined by theorists and suggest teachers find multimodal relationships and thinking outside of the box to be important to the success of a multimodal text. (last para.)

Wierszewski points out the ways in which teachers are willing to adapt their thinking, but notes that these criteria for consideration are still underdeveloped. When asking our students to move beyond taking a traditional academic essay and turning it into a webpage or short digital film, we must introduce them to new ways of thinking about mode and media. Thus, as we consider what writers know and are able to do with digital texts, we must recognize that declarative knowledge (the knowledge of "what") and procedural knowledge (the knowledge of "how") are also affected by a knowledge of technology, as well as the capabilities that technology possesses to enhance a piece of digital writing (Hicks, Turner, & Stratton, 2013).

In practice, this means that digital writing tasks cannot be done simply because we have the technology available. Instead, it must be critical and creative work, designed as an assignment that will help students develop particular skills as digital writers. While some assignments will be short, possibly completed in one class session, and others will be long, stretching on for days or even weeks, we must consider the task at hand and how it will be enhanced or changed through the process of digital writing. As I did above, I offer a few specific suggestions here:

- One way to approach this is to invite students to create initial pieces of digital writing that are "low-stakes" entry points into understanding the technology. For instance, if the ultimate goal for students is to design a 1-minute public service announcement video, it is reasonable to give students a short task at the beginning of the unit that is designed to introduce them to the video editing tool. Perhaps you would give them a one-paragraph script, 10 images, and one class session to create a sample PSA. This would introduce them to the tools, allowing those with more experience to mentor those who may have never used the program before, then open up conversations about the affordances and constraints of the technology.

- Another approach would be to provide students with mentor texts, in much the same way that Julie did by choosing Wonderopolis for her students. Perhaps you could have students review an effective public service announcement, digital book trailer, or digital story; then ask them to use their rhetorical knowledge to identify how these exemplars take full advantage of the MAPS heuristic: mode, media, audience, purpose, and situation.

- Finally, when designing assessment criteria for such projects, help students understand that use of digital writing should not be a superfluous add-on; instead, it should be central to meaning-making. As we would in any writing conference, ask many questions. For instance, if a student is crafting a digital essay or website with hyperlinks, in what ways do those links support the reader's understanding of the topic? Are the links necessary to click upon in order to make meaning, or are they simply citing material from another source?

Recommendation 3: When assessing and evaluating digital writing, we must account for both process and product (and, if we must, assign a grade for each).

There are echoes of many different teachers' practices in my teaching. By looking carefully and describing student work through this reflective process, my practice now includes many chances for students to reflect on how they make community. Screencasts are an important way we share our reflections with each other. We take time to listen to each other describe "how" we made the work. This focus on process has also impacted how I assess student work. I just started teaching at an International Baccalaureate (IB) school and the focus on the Approaches to Learning in the IB curriculum further supports giving student's feedback about the processes they used to create their work.

—Christina Puntel

As anyone familiar with writing pedagogy knows, teachers and researchers of writing have long advocated for a process-oriented approach in our instruction, yet the ideal balance is difficult to strike. As Stephanie's example with Zeke demonstrates, a final product can look very strong, yet the process used to create it may not be what the teacher had hoped for.

Moreover, as Reilly and Atkins (2013) argue, "aspirational assessment" should demonstrate how

> our writing pedagogy values process; therefore, the process of developing, planning, and executing a digital project should be weighed as part of the final product. In the case of completing digital writing projects, this process generally involves risk-taking and experimentation, for which our assessment practices should also account.

This is where it makes sense to connect back to the context and habits of mind found in the Multimodal Assessment Project and the Framework for Success in Postsecondary Writing. By offering students language to discuss their writing processes, we can make our expectations clear, as well as our assessments. VanKooten offers a recursive model that invites students and instructors alike into a dialogue about both process and product (2013). Her "New Media Assessment Model" includes a goal-setting task for writers to begin, considerations of both rhetorical and technical features of the composition, and employment of "multifaceted logic by integrating layers of media such as visuals, sounds, music, animations, written text, and more." Reilly and Atkins, as well as VanKooten, remind us that writers must make decisions about how their compositions will work, anticipating the needs of an audience and constantly striving to meet a particular purpose. By reflecting on the process of composition, as well as on the product, we can invite our students to become better writers in both traditional academic texts and digital pieces.

In practice, this means that assessment becomes an ongoing, formative process. Though we all know that spending our weekends grading papers only to watch students throw our careful comments away on Monday morning is a futile task, we continue to repeat it, hoping that somehow this model of assessment will invite changes in our students' writing process. Not that we ever did, but we certainly no longer have the time or luxury to be able to do this. Put another way, as a teacher of writing, I should be spending 90% of my time coaching my writers and providing feedback before the final grade, and that happens both face-to-face and through virtual interactions including comments, voice messages, and supervision of peer response. Only 10% of my time should be spent in final evaluation and grading. Comments there should be minimal, noting what you have seen in students' work as they have striven to meet their own goals. A few final suggestions:

- One tool that I found useful for creating a basic list of both process- and product-oriented goals is Bernajean Porter's interactive scoring guide tool (Porter, n.d.a; Porter, n.d.b). With these guides, you can choose a particular type of project (e.g., public service announcements or persuasive essays) and then select particular criteria that fall under broad categories of process management and specific traits of the product. She also employs the term "craftsmanship of communication" as a way to discuss how the digital writer uses voice, images, design principles, and interactivity. While the rubrics that this interactive form creates are simple, those rubrics will provide you with a basic set of guidelines that you and your students can then collaboratively build from.

- Use screencasting and screen capture software as tools for students to document their writing process. There are a variety of free options (like Skitch, Jing, Screenr, and QuickTime) as well as more sophisticated programs (such as Camtasia and Snagit) that students can use. For a more detailed example of how students can reflect on their reading and writing process with such tools, I suggest viewing my article "Guiding Student Writers as They Work with Digital Tools" on the MiddleWeb blog (Hicks, 2014).

- Finally—though it is well beyond the scope of one short paragraph to fully explain how and why you might begin using them—I strongly encourage you to work with your colleagues and discuss the option of integrating digital portfolios across the curriculum. As students create digital texts in different classes and over the years of their academic career, they can use a digital portfolio to house the artifact itself, as well as their written or recorded reflections. Then, periodically, as part of a thoughtful review of their existing work, you can guide them to think about how they have employed habits of mind for successful writing and have become more attuned to various modes, media, audiences, and purposes. With digital tools, a portfolio will be much easier to manage over a students' K–12 career than any binder ever was.

As this chapter and entire collection come to a close, please know that I offer these suggestions in the same spirit with which I have worked with Erin, Julie, Jeremy, Bonnie and Jack, Christina, and Stephanie: as one teacher researcher offering possibilities, not as an educational researcher dictating to teachers what they should or should not do in their classrooms. What we have shared here—with our protocol, our student examples, and these suggestions—are ways for you and your colleagues to begin the conversation about teaching digital writing. My hope is that by examining your own students' work, you will take time to look closely, as we have, and to learn as much from the process of composing digital writing as your students have to teach you.

References

Abu El-Haj, T. (2003). Constructing ideas about equity from the standpoint of the particular: Exploring the work of one urban teacher network. *Teachers College Record, 105*(5), 817–845.

Allen, D., & Blythe, T. (2004). *The facilitator's book of questions: Tools for looking together at student and teacher work.* New York, NY: Teachers College Press.

Allison, J., & Gediman, D. (2007). *This I believe: The personal philosophies of remarkable men and women.* New York, NY: Holt Paperbacks.

Alterman, K. [Director]. (2008). *Semi-Pro* [Motion picture]. United States: New Line Cinema.

Banks, A. J. (2010). *Digital griots: African American rhetoric in a multimedia age.* Carbondale, IL: Southern Illinois University Press.

Beers, K., & Probst, R. E. (2012). *Notice and note: Strategies for close reading.* Portsmouth, NH: Heinemann.

Bigelow, B., & Christensen, L. (2001, Winter). Promoting social imagination through interior monologues. *National Writing Project.* Available at nwp. org/cs/public/print/resource/346

Brannon, L., & Knoblauch, C. H. (1982). On students' rights to their own texts: A model of teacher response. *College Composition and Communication, 33*(2), 157. doi:10.2307/357623

Buchanan, J. (1994). Teacher as learner: Working in a community of teachers. In T. Shanahan (Ed.), *Teachers thinking, teachers knowing: Reflections on literacy and language education* (pp. 39–52). Urbana, IL: National Council of Teachers of English.

Caplan, J. (2006). *Time for kids: Volcanoes!* New York, NY: HarperCollins.

Carini, P. F. (2001). *Starting strong: A different look at children, schools, and standards.* New York, NY: Teachers College Press.

Carini, P. F. (2011). Descriptive review of works: Guidelines for describing visual works. In L. Stried (Ed.), *Prospect's descriptive processes: The child, the art of teaching, and the classroom and the school* (rev. ed., pp. 37–40). North Bennington, VT: The Prospect Archives and Center for Education and Research.

Chiseri-Strater, E., & Sunstein, B. S. (2006). *What works?: A practical guide for teacher research.* Portsmouth, NH: Heinemann.

Christensen, L. (2000). *Reading, writing, and rising up: Teaching about social justice and the power of the written word.* Milwaukee, WI: Rethinking Schools

Cochran-Smith, M., & Lytle, S. L. (1992). *Inside/outside: Teacher research and knowledge.* New York, NY: Teachers College Press.

Cochran-Smith, M., & Lytle, S. L. (2009). *Inquiry as stance: Practitioner research in the next generation.* New York, NY: Teachers College Press.

Condie, A. (2013). *Crossed.* New York, NY: Speak.

Costa, A., & Kallick, B. (2000). *Discovering and exploring habits of mind.* Alexandria, VA: Association for Supervision and Curriculum Development.

Council of Writing Program Administrators (CWPA). (2008). WPA outcomes statement for first-year composition. Available at www.in.gov/che/files/WPA_Outcomes_Statement_for_First-Year_Composition.pdf

Council of Writing Program Administrators (CWPA), National Council of Teachers of English (NCTE), & National Writing Project (NWP). (2011, January). Framework for success in postsecondary writing. Available at wpacouncil.org/framework/

Danielewicz, J., & Elbow, P. (2009). A unilateral grading contract to improve learning and teaching. *College Composition and Communication, 61*(2), 244–268.

Derecho, A. T. (2008). *Illegitimate media: Race, gender and censorship in digital remix culture* (Doctoral dissertation, Northwestern University, Evanston, IL). Available at pqdtopen.proquest.com/doc/304541549.html?FMT=AI

Dohn, N. B. (2009). Web 2.0: Inherent tensions and evident challenges for education. *Computer-Supported Collaborative Learning, 4*(3), 343–363. DOI: 10.1007/s11412-009-9066-8

Dubisar, A. M., & Palmeri, J. (2010). Palin/pathos/Peter Griffin: Political video remix and composition pedagogy. *Computers and Composition, 27*(2), 77–93. doi:10.1016/j.compcom.2010.03.004

Fleischer, C. (1995). *Composing teacher-research: A prosaic history.* Albany, NY: State University of New York Press.

Fletcher, R. (2011). *Mentor author, mentor texts.* Portsmouth, NH: Heinemann

Freire, P. (2013). *Pedagogy of freedom: Ethics, democracy, and civic courage* (P. Clarke, trans.). Lanham, MD: Rowman & Littlefield. (Original work published 1997 as *Pedagogía de la autonomía: Saberes necesarios para la práctica educativa*)

Gallagher, C. W. (2014). Staging encounters: Assessing the performance of context in students' multimodal writing. *Computers and Composition, 31,* 1–12. Available at sciencedirect.com/science/article/pii/S8755461513000741

Gallagher, K. (2009). *Readicide: How schools are killing reading and what you can do about it.* Portland, ME: Stenhouse.

Gardner, T. (2008). *Designing writing assignments.* Urbana, IL: National Council of Teachers of English.

Gee, J. P. (2003). *What video games have to teach us about learning and literacy.* New York, NY: Palgrave Macmillan.

Gee, J. P. (2011). Games and learning: Teaching as designing. Available at www. huffingtonpost.com/james-gee/games-and-learning-teachi_b_851581. html

Goswami, D., Lewis, C., Rutherford, M., & Waff, D. (2009). *On teacher inquiry: Approaches to language and literacy research*. New York, NY: Teachers College Press.

Goswami, D., & Stillman, P. (1987). *Reclaiming the classroom: Teacher research as an agency for change*. Upper Montclair, NJ: Boynton/Cook.

Graham, S., & Perin, D. (2007). Writing next: Effective strategies to improve writing of adolescents in middle and high schools—A report to Carnegie Corporation of New York. Washington, DC: Alliance for Excellent Education. Available at all4ed.org/wp-content/uploads/2006/10/WritingNext.pdf

Gura, M. (2014). *Teaching literacy in the digital age: Inspiration for all levels and literacies*. Eugene, OR: International Society for Technology in Education.

Gutiérrez, K. D. (2008). Developing a sociocritical literacy in the third space. *Reading Research Quarterly, 43*(2), 148–164. doi:10.1598/RRQ.43.2.3

Haswell, R. (2006). The complexities of responding to student writing; or, looking for shortcuts via the road of excess. *Across the Disciplines, 3*. Available at wac.colostate.edu/atd/articles/haswell2006.cfm

Hattie, J. (2008). *Visible learning: A synthesis of over 800 meta-analyses relating to achievement*. New York, NY: Routledge.

Heritage, H. M. (2010). *Formative assessment: Making it happen in the classroom*. Thousand Oaks, CA: Corwin.

Herrick, J. W. (2002). Telling stories: Rethinking the personal narrative in the contact zone of a multicultural classroom. In J. M. Wolff (Ed.), *Professing in the contact zone: Bringing theory and practice together* (pp. 274–290). Urbana, IL: National Council of Teachers of English.

Herrington, A., Hodgson, K., & Moran, C. (2009). *Teaching the new writing: Technology, change, and assessment in the 21st-century classroom*. New York, NY: Teachers College Press.

Hicks, T. (2009). *The digital writing workshop*. Portsmouth, NH: Heinemann.

Hicks, T. (2013). *Crafting digital writing: Composing texts across media and genres*. Portsmouth, NH: Heinemann.

Hicks, T. (2014). Guiding student writers as they work with digital tools. Available at www.middleweb.com/14915/digital-writing-student-perspective/

Hicks, T., & Turner, K. H. (2013). No longer a luxury: Digital literacy can't wait. *English Journal, 102*(6), 58–65.

Hicks, T., Turner, K. H., & Stratton, J. (2013). Reimagining a writer's process through digital storytelling. *LEARNing Landscapes, 6*(2), 167–183.

Himley, M., Strieb, L., Carini, P., Kanevsky, R., & Wice, B. (Eds.). (2011). *Prospect's descriptive processes: The child, the art of teaching, and the classroom and school* (rev. ed.). North Bennington, VT: The Prospect Archives and Center for Education and Research. Available at cdi.uvm.edu/resources/ ProspectDescriptiveProcessesRevEd.pdf

Hinton, S. E. (1967). *The outsiders*. New York, NY: Viking Press.

Hyler, J., & Hicks, T. (2014). *Create, compose, connect! Reading, writing, and learning with digital tools*. New York, NY: Routledge.

International Literacy Association. (2009). New literacies and 21st-century technologies. Available at reading.org/general/AboutIRA/PositionStatements/21stCenturyLiteracies.aspx

Ito, M., Gutiérrez, K., Livingstone, S., Penuel, B., Rhodes, J., Salen, K., Schor, J., Sefton-Green, J., & Watkins, S. C. (2013). *Connected learning: An agenda for research and design* (a research synthesis report of the Connected Learning Research Network). Available at dmlhub.net/wp-content/uploads/files/Connected_Learning_report.pdf

Jenkins, H. (2009). *Confronting the challenges of participatory culture: Media education for the 21st century*. Cambridge, MA: The MIT Press.

Jules, G. (2006). Mad world (Tears for Fears cover). On *Trading Snakeoil for Wolftickets* (CD). Selangor Darul Ehsan, Malaysia: Universal Music Ltd. (Malaysia branch). Available at www.last.fm/music/Gary+Jules/_/Mad+World+(Tears+for+Fears+Cover)

King, M. L., Jr. (1967, December 24). A Christmas sermon. Available at www.thekingcenter.org/archive/document/christmas-sermon

Kirby, D. L., & Crovitz, D. (2012). *Inside out: Strategies for teaching writing* (4th ed.). Portsmouth, NH: Heinemann.

Kittle, P. (2008). *Write beside them: Risk, voice, and clarity in high school writing*. Portsmouth, NH: Heinemann.

Kittle, P. (2013). *Book love: Developing depth, stamina, and passion in adolescent readers*. Portsmouth, NH: Heinemann.

Knobel, M., & Lankshear, C. (2006). Profiles and perspectives: Discussing new literacies. *Language Arts, 84*, 78–86.

Lankshear, C. (2004). *A handbook for teacher research: From design to implementation*. Maidenhead, England: Open University Press.

Lehman, C. (2012). *Energize research reading and writing: Fresh strategies to spark interest, develop independence, and meet key common core standards, grades 4–8*. Portsmouth, NH: Heinemann.

Lessig, L. (2008). *Remix: Making art and commerce thrive in the hybrid economy*. New York, NY: Penguin Press.

Literacy Design Collaborative (LDC). (2014). LDC big bank secondary task templates. Available at ldc.org/resources#LDC-Big-Task-Bank

MacLean, M. S., Mohr, M. M., & National Writing Project (U.S.). (1999). *Teacher-researchers at work*. Berkeley, CA: National Writing Project.

McGonigal, J. (2010). Gaming can make a better world [Video file]. Available at ted.com/talks/jane_mcgonigal_gaming_can_make_a_better_world

McKee, H. A., & DeVoss, D. N. (Eds.). (2013). *Digital writing assessment and evaluation*. Logan, UT: Computers and Composition Digital Press/Utah State University Press. Available at ccdigitalpress.org/dwae/index.html

Mezzacappa, D. (2010, October 1). New data: Only 10% of Philly students earn a degree. Available at thenotebook.org/october-2010/102930/new-data-only-10-philly-students-earn-degree

Mohr, M. M. (2004). *Teacher research for better schools*. New York, NY: Teachers College Press; Berkeley, CA: National Writing Project, University of California.

Moline, S. (2011). *I see what you mean: Visual literacy, K–8* (2nd ed.). Portland, ME: Stenhouse.

Moran, C., & Herrington, A. (2013). Seeking guidance for assessing digital compositions/composing. In H. A. McKee & D. N. DeVoss (Eds.), *Digital writing assessment and evaluation* (Chapter 3). Logan, UT: Computers and Composition Digital Press/Utah State University Press. Available at ccdigitalpress.org/dwae/03_moran.html

Multimodal Assessment Project (MAP) Group. (2013). Developing domains for multimodal writing assessment: The language of evaluation, the language of instruction. In H. A. McKee & D. N. DeVoss (Eds.), *Digital writing assessment and evaluation* (Chapter 7). Logan, UT: Computers and Composition Digital Press/Utah State University Press. Available at ccdigitalpress.org/dwae/07_nwp.html

National Association for Media Literacy Education. (2007, November). Core principles of media literacy education in the United States. Available at namle.net/wp-content/uploads/2013/01/CorePrinciples.pdf

National Council of Teachers of English (NCTE). (2007). 21st century literacies: A policy research brief produced by the National Council of Teachers of English. Available at ncte.org/library/NCTEFiles/Resources/PolicyResearch/21stCenturyResearchBrief.pdf

National Council of Teachers of English (NCTE). (2013, November). NCTE framework for 21st century curriculum and assessment: Adopted by the NCTE Executive Committee November 19, 2008. Available at ncte.org/governance/21stcenturyframework?source=gs

National Writing Project (NWP), DeVoss, D., Eidman-Aadahl, E., & Hicks, T. (2010). *Because digital writing matters: Improving student writing in online and multimedia environments*. San Francisco, CA: Jossey-Bass.

National Writing Project & Nagin, C. (2006). *Because writing matters: Improving student writing in our schools* (rev. ed.). San Francisco, CA: Jossey-Bass.

Navas, E. (2006). Remix defined. Available at remixtheory.net/?page_id=3

NCTE Assessment Task Force. (2013). *Formative assessment that truly informs instruction*. Urbana, IL: National Council of Teachers of English.

Neal, M. (2010). *Writing assessment and the revolution in digital texts and technologies*. New York, NY: Teachers College Press.

Newkirk, T., & Kittle, P. (2013). *Children want to write: Donald Graves and the revolution in children's writing*. Portsmouth, NH: Heinemann.

Pink, D. H. (2011). *Drive: The surprising truth about what motivates us.* New York, NY: Riverhead Books.

Popham, W. J. (2008). *Transformative assessment.* Alexandria, VA: Association for Supervision & Curriculum Development.

Porter, B. (n.d.a). Evaluating projects. Available at digitales.us/evaluating-projects

Porter, B. (n.d.b). Scoring guides. Available at digitales.us/evaluating-projects/scoring-guides

Pratt, M. L. (1991). Arts of the contact zone. *Profession 1991, 33–40* (New York, NY: Modern Language Association of America).

Prospect Archive of Children's Work. (n.d.). Iris. Available at cdi.uvm.edu/collections/getCollection.xql?pid=iris&title=(Iris)

Ravitch, D. (2011). *The death and life of the great American school system: How testing and choice are undermining education.* New York, NY: Basic Books.

Ravitch, D. (2013). *Reign of error: The hoax of the privatization movement and the danger to America's public schools.* New York, NY: Knopf.

Ray, K. W. (1999). *Wondrous words: Writers and writing in the elementary classroom.* Urbana, IL: National Council of Teachers of English.

Ray, K. W. (2006). *Study driven: A framework for planning units of study in the writing workshop.* Portsmouth, NH: Heinemann.

Ray, R. E. (1996). Afterword: Ethics and representation in teacher research. In P. Mortensen & G. Kirsch (Eds.), *Ethics and representation in qualitative studies of literacy* (pp. 287–300). Urbana, IL: National Council of Teachers of English.

Reep, Z. (2012, November 16). Forgiveness-1ZR [Video file]. Available at youtube.com/watch?v=22N1gGapvts&feature=youtube_gdata_player

Reilly, C. A., & Atkins, A. T. (2013). Rewarding risk: Designing aspirational assessment processes for digital writing projects. In H. A. McKee & D. N. DeVoss (Eds.), *Digital writing assessment and evaluation* (Chapter 4). Logan, UT: Computers and Composition Digital Press/Utah State University Press. Available at ccdigitalpress.org/dwae/04_reilly.html

Richardson, W. (2012). *Why school? How education must change when learning and information are everywhere* [Kindle single]. New York, NY: TED Conferences. Available at amazon.com.

Sarah Lawrence College. (2011, November 8). 25th anniversary tribute to the art of teaching program by Patricia Carini [Video file]. Available at www.youtube.com/watch?v=IHUSwhAOEmY&feature=youtube_gdata_player

Seif, E. (2009, July). A school for peace and justice. *Educational Leadership, 66.* Available at ascd.org/publications/educational-leadership/jul09/vol66/num10/A-School-for-Peace-and-Justice.aspx

Selber, S. (2004). *Multiliteracies for a digital age.* Carbondale, IL: Southern Illinois University Press.

Shaughnessy, M. P. (1977). *Errors and expectations: A guide for the teacher of basic writing.* New York, NY: Oxford University Press.

Spandel, V. (2005). *Creating writers through 6-trait writing assessment and instruction* (4th ed.). Boston, MA: Pearson Allyn and Bacon.

Stedman, K. D. (2012). Remix literacy and fan compositions. *Computers and Composition, 29*(2), 107–123. doi:10.1016/j.compcom.2012.02.002

Stock, P. L. (1995). *The dialogic curriculum: Teaching and learning in a multicultural society.* Portsmouth, NH: Heinemann.

Stock, P. L. (2001). Toward a theory of genre in teacher research: Contributions from a reflective practitioner. *English Education, 33*(2), 100–114.

Tchudi, S. (Ed.), & NCTE Committee on Alternatives to Grading Student Writing. (1997). *Alternatives to grading student writing.* Urbana, IL: National Council of Teachers of English.

United Nations. (2008). United Nations Millennium Development Goals. Available at un.org/millenniumgoals/.

VanKooten, C. (2013). Toward a rhetorically sensitive assessment model for new media composition. In H. A. McKee & D. N. DeVoss (Eds.), *Digital writing assessment and evaluation* (Chapter 9). Logan, UT: Computers and Composition Digital Press/Utah State University Press. Available at ccdigitalpress.org/dwae/09_vankooten.html

Warschauer, M. (2011). *Learning in the cloud: How (and why) to transform schools with digital media.* New York, NY: Teachers College Press.

What Works Clearinghouse. (2002). Does not meet evidence screens. Available at w-w-c.org/reviewprocess/notmeetscreens.html

Whithaus, C. (2014, March). Letter from the editor. *Computers and Composition, 31*, v–ix.

Wierszewski, E. (2013). "Something old, something new": Evaluative criteria in teacher responses to student multimodal texts. In H. A. McKee & D. N. DeVoss (Eds.), *Digital writing assessment and evaluation* (Chapter 5). Logan, UT: Computers and Composition Digital Press/Utah State University Press. Available at ccdigitalpress.org/dwae/05_wierszewski.html

Wiggins, G. P., & McTighe. J. (2005). *Understanding by design* (expanded 2nd ed.). Alexandria, VA: Association for Supervision and Curriculum Development.

Wilhelm, J. D., & Novak, B. (2011). *Teaching literacy for love and wisdom: Being the book and being the change.* New York, NY: Teachers College Press.

Wysocki, A. F., & Lynch, D. A. (2007). *Compose, design, advocate: A rhetoric for integrating written, visual, and oral communication.* New York, NY: Longman.

Index

About the Contributors

Dr. Troy Hicks is an associate professor of English at Central Michigan University and focuses his work on the teaching of writing, literacy, and technology, and teacher education and professional development. Hicks directs CMU's Chippewa River Writing Project, a site of the National Writing Project, and he frequently conducts professional development workshops related to writing and technology. Follow him on Twitter @hickstro.

Jeremy Hyler is a 7th/8th-grade teacher at Fulton Middle School in Michigan. He is also a codirector of the Chippewa River Writing Project. Hyler has authored multiple chapters in professional texts and co-authored *Create, Compose, Connect! Reading, Writing, and Learning with Digital Tools* (2014) with Dr. Troy Hicks. In addition to his writings, he has presented at professional conferences in the state of Michigan, as well as at the national level.

Julie Johnson is a literacy coach and reading intervention specialist in Hilliard City Schools. A National Board Certified teacher, she has taught a variety of grades in elementary school. She participated in the summer institute with the Columbus Area Writing Project in 2007 and received NCTE's Donald Graves Excellence in Teaching Writing award in 2010.

Bonnie Kaplan taught high school English and Drama for 30 years and loved every minute of her work in the classroom and with her students onstage. For the last 15 years she's been a codirector of the Hudson Valley Writing Project, and her work both locally and nationally has offered her unique opportunities to work with amazing teachers, like the group that collaborated on this book. She watched her first digital story at a National Writing Project institute in 2003 and the experience was transformative. In her spare time she travels, plays classical guitar, and loves to catch a movie on its opening weekend.

Erin Klein is an award-winning educator, national keynote speaker, author, and mother who has been twice selected to serve on the Scholastic, Inc. Top Teaching Team based in New York. Her recent publication, *Amazing Grades*, was a collaboration with experts from 13 countries around the world. She travels the country speaking about the power of student voice, how meaningful technology integration can enhance learning experiences, and the impact classroom design has on today's learner. She has her Master's of Education in Curriculum and Instruction, currently teaches at the elementary level, and lives in Michigan with her family. Her work can be found on her award-winning educational blog, Kleinspiration.com, and you can follow her on Twitter @KleinErin.

Christina Puntel is a Spanish teacher at Hill Freedman World Academy in Philadelphia. A teacher since 1998, she was raised by two strong teacher inquiry groups, the Philadelphia Teachers' Learning Cooperative (PTLC) and the Philadelphia Writing Project. Her practice has been influenced by the processes of PTLC and the Prospect Center in Vermont. She loves the space that the act of making, both digitally and by hand, affords her students in her language classes. *¡Qué viva la creatividad!*

Stephanie West-Puckett teaches writing at East Carolina University, where she is also pursuing a doctoral degree in Writing, Rhetoric, and Professional Communication. She is associate director of the Tar River Writing Project, and her research explores the intersections of digital literacies and feminist/queer theories in formal and informal educational spaces.

Jack Zangerle works as an English teacher at Dover Plains Middle School in Dover Plains, NY, where he also serves as the department chair. Exploring the intersection of education and technology is a passion for him. Zangerle is a teacher consultant for the Hudson Valley Writing Project, and he also works as an adjunct professor at Marist College.